THE TWILIGHT COMPANION

the
twilight
companion

the unauthorized guide
to the series

✧

lois h. gresh

st. martin's griffin ❧ new york

www.stmartins.com

ISBN-13: 978-0-312-38705-1
ISBN-10: 0-312-38705-9

First Edition: November 2008

10 9 8 7 6 5 4 3 2 1

To vampire fans everywhere!

CONTENTS

chapter 1   I Beg You: Please Suck My Blood   *1*

chapter 2   Sexy Vampires: They're Beautiful, Strong,   *15*
and Immortal, So What's Not to Like?

chapter 3   What to Expect When You Fall in Love with   *28*
a Vampire

chapter 4   Bella's Awakening: What Really Happens When   *38*
You Turn into a Vampire

chapter 5   Vampire Quiz!   *49*

chapter 6   Good Vampires and Bad Vampires   *63*

chapter 7   Sexy Werewolves: They're Furry, Strong,   *77*
and Sensitive New Age Kinds of Guys, So
What's Not to Like?

chapter 8   What to Expect When You Fall in Love with   *86*
a Werewolf

chapter 9   Werewolf Quiz!   *92*

chapter 10   Good Werewolves and Bad Werewolves   *96*

chapter 11   Vampires and Werewolves: Can They *Ever* Be   *105*
Friends?

chapter 12   Favorite Twilight Characters and Vampires and   *112*
Werewolves Throughout Time

chapter 13   Protecting Your Vampire, Part 1: Everything You   *119*
Need to Know About Fangs, Sunlight, Crosses,
Garlic, and Holy Water

chapter 14   Protecting Your Vampire, Part 2: Everything You   *141*
Need to Know About Coffins, Black Capes, Bats,
Wooden Stakes Through the Heart, Decapitation,
and Fire

chapter 15   Vampire Test!   *160*

chapter 16   Living Forever: Is It All That It's Cracked   *167*
Up to Be?

chapter 17 Mental Telepathy and Seeing the Future   175

chapter 18 Romance Quiz: Could Edward Be the Man   184
            for You?

chapter 19 The Final Twilight Book: All the Answers You've   234
            Been Dying to Learn

THE TWILIGHT COMPANION

CHAPTER 1

I BEG YOU:
Please Suck My Blood

✧

Throughout the first three books of Stephenie Meyer's extremely popular Twilight Saga, heroine Isabella, aka Bella Swan, desperately wants vampire Edward Cullen to suck her blood. She wants to be a vampire with him, young forever, in love forever, and for that to happen requires that Edward mix his blood with hers and taint her with the gift (or curse) of vampirism.

It's a theme of many vampire movies and books, though in the case of Twilight, it's done a little differently. Bella's vampire friends, the Cullens, aren't like other vampires we've met, nor are her werewolf friends like the werewolves we've encountered in other tales.

These vampires and werewolves have souls and consciences. They care about humans. They don't want to kill people, and indeed, they will sacrifice themselves to protect their human loved ones.

In most vampire lore, the blood-sucking guy doesn't have much in the way of compassion. He can't resist slurping up as much blood as possible from the necks of beautiful, young women—men and children as well, though most traditional vampires seem to have a preference for the blood of young women. It's alluring to them, just as the young women find the vampires highly alluring.

It's as if the vampire grabs hold of the girl, her very soul, and she can't escape his clutches. This is the typical way of the vampire, whether he's a creepy, ancient, gnarled monster as in the 1922 film *Nosferatu*, which I'll tell you about later in this book, or a suave, handsome charmer like Bela Lugosi, who starred in the 1931 version of Bram Stoker's *Dracula*. Of course, there are the in-between vampires, who are actually disgusting, batlike, ancient monsters who can *look* like young, handsome guys whenever they want. One example is Dracula in the 1992 Francis Ford Coppola film *Bram Stoker's Dracula*.

Don't worry. I'll tell you all about these various other vampires in this book, and then, we can compare them to Edward Cullen and his family. What does Edward have in common with the original Count Dracula and all of the other vampires who came before him? How is his family different from theirs? Historically, do vampires and werewolves fight as they do in the Twilight Saga, or are they friends? These are only some of the questions we'll answer in this book.

But of all the questions we contemplate, perhaps the most burning one is: What is it about Edward Cullen that makes him so desirable, hot, and sexy?

At seventeen, if you encountered Edward Cullen in your biology class, would you fall for him? If you saw him in the school cafeteria, would you instantly be drawn to him? Probably. I know I would! After all, Stephenie Meyer describes him as "devastatingly, inhumanly beautiful."[1]

As for Bella Swan, what girl wouldn't want to be her?

Here she is, an ordinary gal, moving to some godforsaken, gloomy, remote town to live with her father. Her mother has re-

---

1. Stephenie Meyer, *Twilight* (New York: Little, Brown and Company, 2005), p. 19.

married, and it's time for Bella to give her mom some space. Now, I don't know many girls who leave home to live with fathers they don't know just to give their remarried mothers space, but Bella is special.

So she moves to Forks, Washington, where it always rains, and while attending the small rural school as the new kid, *bam*, she snags Edward Cullen, an incredibly handsome dude with the most appealing personality you could possibly imagine. You may know what this is like: you see a guy, and he has the sweetest smile and a shy way about him, yet you can tell that he also has the hots for you. You get to know him, and not only is he madly in love with you, basically worshipping the ground you walk on, but he's compassionate, understanding, kind, and wonderful in all ways. He is Mr. Perfect. Any girl would want this guy, and any girl would want to be Bella, who is the object of Edward's desires.

MR. PERFECT

Every girl wants to meet Mr. Perfect, and every girl has her own image of what Mr. Perfect will be like. Most of us want to be with a guy who makes us laugh, understands us, forgives our shortcomings, and thinks we're the most beautiful and wonderful girl on Earth. Most girls would add that Mr. Perfect must be physically attractive, but of course, that attribute differs depending on the girl to whom you're talking.

Popular magazines survey women and then list the top ten most attractive men on a yearly basis. *People* magazine actually calls their list "Top 10 Sexiest Men Alive." In

(continued)

2007, *People* magazine[2] identified these guys as the top ten sexiest:

1. Thirty-seven-year-old Matt Damon, a famous movie star (*The Bourne Ultimatum, The Good Shepherd*, etc.), was selected as top choice because of his good sense of humor, his stay-at-home family man attitude, and his humble attitude.
2. Forty-one-year-old Patrick Dempsey, who stars on the television program *Grey's Anatomy*, has been married for eight years (yes, to the same girl) and has three children. The magazine doesn't state why Dempsey's on the list, but on the surface, he seems to have family values in common with Matt Damon. The magazine does quote him as saying that eyes are the most attractive part of a woman, which implies that he might be a sensitive, compassionate sort of guy.
3. Thirty-one-year-old Canadian movie star Ryan Reynolds (*X-Men Origins: Wolverine, The Amityville Horror*, etc.), who apparently is on the list for his physical charms: he's six feet two inches tall with rock-hard muscles. Edward Cullen is tall, handsome, and has rock-hard muscles, too.
4. Forty-three-year-old extremely famous movie star Brad Pitt (*Troy, Mr. & Mrs. Smith, Fight Club*, etc.), who is described as handsome.
5. Twenty-eight-year-old James McAvoy, who starred in the movie *Atonement*, in which his character was madly in love with his girlfriend and nobody else—forever. Hence, he also has something in common with Edward Cullen.
6. Forty-four-year-old extremely famous movie star Johnny Depp (*Pirates of the Caribbean, Edward Scissorhands*,

---

2. http://www.people.com/people/package/gallery/0,,20154290_20159879,00 .html.

etc.), who is supposedly appealing because he's unusual and doesn't care what other people think of him and how he lives. He's also described by the magazine as being a family man.

7. Twenty-eight-year-old television and movie actor Dave Annable (*Brothers & Sisters* TV series, etc.), who is pictured cuddling up to an extremely cute dog.

8. Thirty-nine-year-old extremely famous movie star Will Smith (*I Am Legend, Men in Black*, etc.), who is described as the ultimate family man, in love with his wife and only his wife—forever.

9. Thirty-eight-year-old Spanish actor Javier Bardem (*No Country for Old Men, Love in the Time of Cholera*, etc.) who possesses a "seductive intensity."

10. Thirty-seven-year-old Shemar Moore, a former soap opera star/model who claims that his sex appeal has a lot do with his haircut, his tan, and his clothing.

One thing that really sticks out about all ten of *People* magazine's sexiest men alive is that they are much older than Edward Cullen. This means that the women compiling the list (or voting for the sexiest men alive) are not in high school like Bella. Maybe a forty-four-year-old family man is sexy to a mother in her late thirties. Maybe a guy in his thirties or forties who is faithful to his wife and children, and who happens to be a handsome, wealthy movie star, is the ideal sexy guy for a lady who is also in her thirties or forties.

But where are the *young* guys on this list? Let's review just a few young guys who are movie stars and see if they are as appealing to us as Edward Cullen. First, there's Daniel Radcliffe,

(continued)

who is nineteen years old and the star of the *Harry Potter* movies. Does he appeal to you more than Edward Cullen? My guess is that you're shaking your head no. Edward has those muscles, that smile, those eyes, that intensely passionate way about him.

Then there's a guy named Emile Hirsh, who is twenty-three years old and was in movies such as *The Girl Next Door* (2004). He's definitely cute, but again, Edward Cullen is much sexier.

And there are others, of course. Leonardo DiCaprio comes to mind, but he's thirty-three years old, which puts him way out of the ballpark in competing with the seventeen-year-old Edward Cullen (who was born in 1901, which made him a whopping 104 years old in 2005 when *Twilight* was first published). In terms of movie stars, it's hard to think of anyone who is approximately seventeen years old and who looks, acts, and thinks like Edward Cullen.

Edward *is* Mr. Perfect.

An obvious candidate for *People* magazine's "Top 10 Sexiest Men Alive" list is gorgeous Robert Pattinson, who plays the role of Edward Cullen in the Twilight movie. Born in 1986, Pattinson is an English actor with bronze-brown hair and medium brown eyes, which could look molten bronze with the help of contact lenses.

Bella makes lots of friends, and even has another boy, Mike Newton, constantly chasing her. Mike is cute with light blond hair; he's friendly, and he's extremely attentive and nice to her. Bella doesn't know how to handle Mike because he's attracted to her; she doesn't want to hurt him, yet she's not romantically interested in him.

We all know what this is like and how difficult it is to ease someone away without hurting his feelings. In ninth grade, there was a guy who sat next to me in band, and he ended up asking me to the junior prom. I was horrified because I really didn't know him at all, and he was just a guy sitting next to me in band. It's not as if I daydreamed about him or wanted to get to know him at all. To prove that point, the extent of our conversation had been limited to the following:

"Turn the page."

"Uh-huh."

That was it, turning sheet music to the next page. So I ended up giving an excuse of some kind and not going to the junior prom.

When you're a junior or senior in high school, it's okay to be rejected, if it's done in a kind way. The guys are still resilient, and they just move on and try to score with another chick. They don't hate you for it. They barely remember you after you turn them down.

In the end, Mike doesn't hate Bella for turning him down, either. He pines for her endlessly, but of course, she hooks him up with a friend, and things work out for the best.

Bella is a wonderful character: she's an ordinary kind of girl, just like you and me; she has a nice personality, very caring and considerate; and she's also loyal and devoted. And if that weren't enough in the way of positive characteristics, she's intelligent, too. So who wouldn't want to be like Bella?

✧

The book you hold in your hands was written from one Twilight fan to another. I'm assuming you've read all three of Stephenie Meyer's terrific books in the Twilight Saga: *Twilight, Eclipse,* and

New Moon. I'm also assuming that, by the time this book is in print, you might already be holding her fourth Twilight book and turning to page one. I bought it and read it as soon as it was available. After all, I wanted to know if Edward gives Bella her dream, to be a vampire and "live" with him forever. Or if maybe, Edward found a way to be human again, just seventeen, so he and Bella could truly live happily ever after, though not forever. This is what we were all dying (sorry to use that word when writing about Bella and vampires) to know.

But there are other matters at hand. For example, reading the first three Twilight books, especially the first one, made me start wondering, just what is it that attracts us girls to these gorgeous guys? Why can't we resist molten copper eyes and big muscles? Why is it so important that we feel special to our guys? Remember, Edward's been "alive" for more than a hundred years, yet he's never fallen in love, not until he runs into Bella Swan, that is. Stephenie Meyer has us all wondering: why is Bella so special to Edward? This book is going to delve into these questions, guiding you through vampire lore, seeking to discover whether vampires have always been this way with their girls, or if it's only Edward who falls in love once—with Bella.

We'll also think about vampires themselves and why they've appealed to women throughout the ages. I'd rather think that we are mesmerized by them than think that we all want our blood drained. But honestly, unless it's a real vampire with those intoxicating eyes and supernatural powers, this remains a very valid question. Since Bela Lugosi in the 1931 Dracula film, women have been glued to vampire movies and books, and there has to be a reason. We'll attempt to figure out what that reason might be.

If you fall in love with a vampire, you don't have a rule book to follow. Your mother can't give you advice, and neither can your dad. There's no book telling the new bride of a vampire what's expected of her, how to act around the in-laws, whether and how she can even have children, and so forth. If you have a baby with your vampire man, there's no baby book or pediatrician equipped to tell you about raising a baby vampire. Can you take the baby to a playground without risking the lives of a bunch of toddlers? I wonder. if vampire babies need milk, or whether a diet of nothing but blood suffices to build strong bones and brains.

HOW MANY PEOPLE DOES A VAMPIRE NEED TO DRINK TO STAY ALIVE?

After sucking blood out of the neck of a young woman, the typical vampire is so full that he nearly collapses. This implies that a thin, young woman has blood containing a lot of nutrition, or at least, a lot of calories.

Let's assume our male vampire has the body and metabolism of a seventeen-year-old, just like Edward Cullen. Let's also assume that he weighs 165 pounds and is only six feet tall, just to keep things simple. Hunting in the forest every night, running close to the speed of light, lifting vans: our vampire dude is in great shape, just like Edward, and has a lot of muscles. We can also say that his activity level is high. This particular type of creature, if he were pure human, might need approximately 3,200 calories per day.

Okay, now let's assume that our male vampire has the body and metabolism of a hundred-year-old, just like Nosferatu in

(continued)

the 1922 film. In this case, we'll assume that he weighs 140 pounds and is only five feet ten inches tall. He's emaciated but still in good shape for such an old guy. He doesn't have much muscle on his vampiric body. His activity level is pretty low, as he seems to stay in his castle most of the time, drinking blood from wine bottles and small animals. He's incredibly bloodthirsty for a young woman, so much so that he travels in a coffin across the ocean simply to pursue someone's wife. If even remotely human, this guy might need 1,200 calories per day.

In each case, we should add vampiric calories to the human calories that we just calculated. For example, a vampire transforms into bats, wolves, and mists, and this must take a lot of energy. I don't know of any medical studies that have established the caloric needs of a shapeshifting creature, so we're in new territory here. Let's say a vampire needs 1,200 calories to transform from human to bat/wolf/mist form, and maybe 1,200 calories to return to his ordinary form. That's a total of 2,400 calories.

The young virile vampire thus needs a total of 3,200 plus 2,400 calories, or 5,600 calories per day. The ancient gnarled Nosferatu type of vampire needs 1,200 plus 2,400 calories, or 3,600 calories per day.

The average person has about 5 liters, or 5,000 milliliters of blood in her body. If you donate a pint of blood, you're donating approximately 473 milliliters of blood. If you pass out, which I have done simply by donating a pint of blood, beware of any vampire. He'll suck out a lot more than one pint. It's amazing that his female victims remain conscious at all.

According to the Mayo Clinic, a person who donates one

pint of blood loses 650 calories.[3] Note to readers on diets: do not donate blood as a method of weight loss. It's not blood you want to remove from your body (if so, get a vampire boyfriend), it's excess fat. What's the point of ending up with a fat body that has no blood in it?

All we need now is a simple calculation, and we'll know how many people a typical vampire needs to suck dry every day. If a typical person has 5,000 milliliters of blood in her body, and each 473 milliliters contain 650 calories, then:

5,000 divided by 473 equals 10.57
10.57 multiplied by 650 calories equals 6,870.50 calories of
blood in a typical human body

It's enough for a vampire like Edward, who might need about 5,600 calories per day, and it's like a couple of Thanksgiving feasts for an ancient wisplike Nosferatu.

I suspect that bears have a lot more blood in them than humans, so if a young male vampire drains a bear every now and then, he can probably remain healthy for a long time. Hence, a male Cullen vampire can probably sustain himself for lengthy periods without draining even one human female.

---

3. http://www.mayoclinic.org/donateblood/know.html.

Beyond all that, which is a lot, if Bella and Edward continue to be a couple, as she desperately wants, she's going to have to learn a lot about protecting her man. Again, there's no guide to the health of a vampire. There's no American Vampire Health Association. No Red Cross for Vampires (though it would be amusing to have a *Red Cross* for them). Heaven knows that no insurance company would give a vampire dental coverage. So, if you fall in love with a vampire boy, you need guidelines about protecting him from crosses, garlic, holy water, and certainly, wooden stakes. You'll have to learn how to sew black capes, or at minimum, where to find the best buys in black capes. Unless your vampire man is more like Edward, who never wears the archetypical vampiric black cape.

We never see Edward sleeping in a coffin, but it's quite possible that, should you fall in love with your own vampire, he's going to want a deluxe coffin. Or at least, a coffin that's comfortable, and remember, his coffin will have to last for hundreds and maybe thousands of years.

And then there are the bats: you'd better get used to them, having hundreds of bats flocking around your head at a moment's notice. Not to mention wolves howling outside your window for the rest of your life. Get used to it.

These are all subjects that I was thinking about as I read the Twilight series. I kept thinking, *Poor Bella, she's in love with a vampire. If Edward doesn't finally turn her into a vampire, too, she's going to have to contend with all of these strange things.*

Now, if Edward does turn Bella into a vampire in the fourth book, then she'll have a host of other, far stranger things with which to contend. What really happens when you're turned into a vampire? We'll attempt to address these sorts of questions, too.

And I'm just touching on the subjects of this book. There are so many more! Such as:

If you're Bella and your man is Edward (or just fill in your name and your boyfriend's name here, and pretend that your real boyfriend is a vampire), well, then, how will you survive Christmas and Easter with him and his family? And what about Halloween? Are you really willing to give up almost all of your favorite holidays to be with this guy?

How can Dr. Cullen, Edward's adoptive father, get away with being a practicing physician when he's really a vampire? It's hard to get and keep a medical license, and the government requires tons of paperwork and validation. Dr. Cullen was born in the 1640s and certified as a physician shortly after transforming into a vampire. My guess is that it would raise a lot of suspicion in medical circles if this guy showed up at Acme Hospital in 2008, seeking a job as a doctor.

Obviously, as Twilight fans, you all know that there's more than vampires to these stories. There's also . . . *Jacob*. He's a werewolf. In fact, his entire family consists of werewolves.

Jacob is Bella's best friend. He really helps her through some very hard times, such as when Edward leaves her for an incredibly long time. Bella professes to love Jacob, though not in the romantic way she loves Edward. Jacob, and even Edward at times, thinks that Jacob is the boy for Bella. Making matters stickier is that, in the Twilight Saga, vampires and werewolves are enemies.

All of this leads me to wonder, as Bella sometimes does, why she seems to fall for monsters instead of ordinary human boys. *What's next?* I wonder. Will a seventeen-year-old Frankenstein monster move to Forks and befriend her?

In real folklore, werewolves are quite different from Jacob and his family, just as in real folklore, vampires are quite different from Edward and the Cullen family. As the vampire craves human blood, so does the werewolf. Both are generally compelled to prey upon those closest to them. A werewolf bite, so goes the popular tale, turns the victim into a werewolf, though most often, werewolves bite to kill and cannibalize their prey. Pretty ugly, huh? It's hard to imagine falling in love or having best friends who are creatures who, after nightfall, attack children and young women, boys and men, and gobble them all up. But in Twilight, both vampire and werewolf are portrayed as more human than monster.

So, if you're a fan of Stephenie Meyer's books, you've come to the right place. Here, you'll find answers to all of your burning questions about vampires and Edward, werewolves and Jacob, and what drives girls like Bella to love them.

CHAPTER 2

SEXY VAMPIRES:
They're Beautiful, Strong, and Immortal, So What's Not to Like?

✧

There's an old and famous theatrical production called *Fiddler on the Roof*, in which girls find their husbands through the efforts of a matchmaker. This matchmaker tends to be an old woman who makes her living by convincing parents to marry off their daughters to the men she picks. I can just picture the *Fiddler on the Roof* matchmaker saying things like, "Listen, Charlie, the boy is wealthy and can take care of your Bella. He's handsome, strong, and intelligent, and he loves her. So what's not to like?"

Of course, Charlie is Bella Swan's father, the police chief of Forks, Washington. Bella's mother, Renée, left Charlie and Forks, and took infant Bella with her to Phoenix, Arizona, where Bella's grown up. My grandmother's name was Rena, which is very similar to Renée, and oddly enough, I had an Uncle Charlie, too. Had I grown up in my grandma Rena's house, then moved in with my uncle Charlie when I was in high school, maybe I could have met a handsome guy like Edward and befriended a family of vampires. Probably not, but the similarity in family names is kind of creepy, don't you think? Of course, my name isn't Bella or Donna, or even Belladonna, it's just plain Lois. On the other hand, when I did get married—long after high school, of course—all the males in my husband's family were named Jake, short for Jacob. I'm not kidding. There was an Earl Jake Senior, Junior, the Third, and even the Fourth, and an Uncle Jake; and all of those Jacobs were just in our immediate family. Please excuse me for a moment, while I check my neck for bite marks.

(pause)

(pause)

Okay, I'm clean. Sorry to delay this chapter to check for family vampire ties, but with so many parallels in family names to Bella's family and friends, I figured it was wise to make sure.

FORKS, WASHINGTON

Forks, Washington, is a real place on the Olympic Peninsula that is named after forks in some nearby rivers, including the Quillayute River and Bogachiel River. While Forks once had a thriving timber business, employment there is now confined mainly to correctional facilities. It's a tiny place, only about three square miles in size. About five percent of the population in Forks is Native American. Sadly, about a fifth of the people in Forks live in poverty, and more than a quarter of the children under eighteen years old are beneath the poverty line.

For Bella to have her own truck, rusty junk heap or not, is lavish in the real Forks, Washington. It's also an extremely odd place for wealthy vampires to hang out and drive expensive cars. Anyone with an expensive car is going to stick out in Forks.

And now for the big question: does it really rain constantly in Forks, Washington? The real Forks *is* overcast and rainy, yes. In fact, the annual town festival is called Rainfest.

So we all know that Bella moves to Forks, where the high school has a total of three hundred and fifty-eight students, including her. This is a small school, no doubt about it. In my class in high school, we had approximately seven hundred kids, and in the entire high school, all grade levels, tenth through twelfth, there were about two thousands kids. Where my own children went to high school, each class had about fifty (my daughter's class) to eighty (my son's class) students, for a grand total of maybe one hundred fifty to two hundred forty kids in the entire high school. Forks High School is about the same size, slightly bigger, than the high school here where I live. *Small.*

And where I live is also a lot *like* Forks. Always overcast, gloomy, rains a lot, has many ice storms.

Given how much I seem to have in common with Bella's family and how my little village is so similar to Forks, it's beginning to feel very odd that I'm not friends with any immortal creatures.

I'd better watch my neck.

In any small town, be it Forks or where I live, the people are a lot like the ones Bella encounters. Everyone knows everyone else. Everyone's grandparents grew up in town. People gossip far too much, and they hold grudges forever, often for generations. Most small towns, granted, don't have werewolves holding grudges against vampire families literally *forever*, but still, the creepy, gloomy, small-town atmosphere that Stephenie Meyer portrays is dead-on accurate. It's part of what makes her novels so intense, so alive, so realistic. It's part of what makes us believe that Edward could be real, and that he and Bella could actually go to school and hang out in Forks just as they do.

Bella first sees the vampire family in school. The boys are all gorgeous. As are the girls. In fact, the entire Cullen family is so exquisite that Bella cannot take her eyes off them. This is common in all vampire movies, in that the human cannot take his or her eyes off the vampires, all of whom are gorgeous.

Bella doesn't know yet that the five Cullen kids are vampires, of course, though it's clear that they all have extremely pale complexions, and dark eyes with purplish bruises beneath them. She thinks of them as having the faces of angels. I rarely think of angels as having purple bruises beneath their eyes, but I do think of angels as having ethereal expressions and pale complexions.

Of course, first and foremost, there's Edward, who was gorgeous even when he was a human with his emerald eyes and bronze-auburn hair. He stands six feet two inches tall, and he's extremely muscular. He's so incredibly handsome that Bella sometimes thinks of him as Michelangelo's David.

I actually saw the statue of David in the Accademia Gallery in Florence, Italy. Even as a statue, David's physique was impressive, to say the least. It was *perfect*. Many experts claim that the statue of David is the most recognizable stone sculpture ever made. It is *the* symbol of youth and beauty.

If Edward looks like the David statue, he does indeed look godlike. Michelangelo's statue of David, the one I actually saw in Italy, was commissioned in 1501 by the Florentine Republic. If you went to religious school, you might remember that David was a biblical hero who defeated the giant named Goliath. In 1504, Michelangelo finished his huge statue, a nude David who looks like a Greek god. In this sculpture, David's muscles are strong and taut, his face is full of both beauty and tension.

Alice Cullen, the vampire sister of Edward, becomes a main character and good friend of Bella's. She was born in 1901, stuck in an insane asylum, and eventually, turned into a vampire. She's pale and petite, with spiked black hair and the grace of a professional dancer. She is portrayed by twenty-one-year-old actress Ashley Greene in the Twilight movie.

Picture a beautiful girl with jet black hair and golden eyes. It's hard to imagine someone that beautiful, isn't it? And now add the charm of being able to move quickly and gracefully, with no effort whatsoever, and you have the image of a girl who is so mesmerizing that any guy would fall for her.

Another vampire in the family, Emmett Cullen, played by Kellan Lutz in the Twilight movie, is extremely tall, muscular, and athletic. He is actually six feet five inches tall, has dimples, golden eyes, and pale skin. Emmett easily could be the romantic hero in his own series, given what he looks like, that is.

And then there's Jasper Hale, played by twenty-three-year-old actor Jackson Rathbone in the Twilight movie, who is also extremely tall and muscular, with the golden eyes of the entire family. And finally, there's Rosalie Hale, described as so shockingly gorgeous that she's a knockout even when compared to other vampires. She is played by beautiful twenty-year-old actress Nikki Reed in the Twilight movie. Take an ordinary blond statuesque goddess-girl—we've all known this type of girl throughout our lives—and now make her especially willowy and tall, graceful and classy, with golden eyes to match waist-length golden hair. I'm thinking of the most beautiful blond girl in my high school class, and stunning as she was, Stephenie Meyer's description of Rosalie makes the vampire girl insanely attractive in comparison. If Rosalie had been in my high school, all the boys would have chased her instead of the pretty blonde who *was* in our class.

This first introduction to the Cullen family marks the vampires

THE MOST BEAUTIFUL WOMEN ALIVE

Earlier, we talked about the ten sexiest men alive, at least according to *People* magazine, and we compared them to Edward. Now, let's peek at some of the so-called sexiest women alive, and see how they measure up to the Cullen girls.

According to *Esquire* magazine, which caters to men, Charlize Theron was the sexiest woman alive in 2007. Charlize is tall and blond, much like Rosalie Cullen.

According to *Glamour* magazine,[1] which caters to women, some of the sexiest women alive in 2007 included tall, blond Scarlett Johansson, but also dark-haired Jessica Alba, supermodel Gisele Bündchen, the *Friends* television-show star Jennifer Aniston, and of course, Angelina Jolie, who seems to top most men's charts of sexy women. Various other models, as well as singers Beyoncé and Jennifer Lopez, also made the *Glamour* list.

Hey, what about eighteen-year-old Kristen Stewart, who is slated (as of this writing) to play the character of Bella Swan in the Twilight movie? She's stunning, with brown hair and greenish eyes. I've always pictured Bella as more plain, but it's nice to think of her as being as gorgeous as Kristen Stewart.

What constitutes beauty is a touchy subject for us girls. We're always told that it's the inner self that matters, and certainly, *People* magazine's choices for sexiest man alive make it clear that the guys are being selected for far more than their looks. Most of the guys on the list are family

---

1. http://www.thinkfashion.com/blogs/stylosity_hollywood_hookup/archive/2007/04/10/glamour-magazine-unveils-hollywood-s-sexiest-women-of-2007.aspx.

men who claim that they will love their wives forever; they're sensitive, sweet, yet macho guys, and sure, they look okay, too.

But we girls are held to different standards, it seems, no matter how much lip talk we've been given about beauty being on the inside. After all, the most sexy women are chosen because they literally are models or glamour babes. The fact that they're faithful to their husbands or that they're good mothers somehow never comes into play when they're chosen for this particular list.

It is a double standard, and it bothers a lot of girls, but luckily, we also know that what's inside does indeed matter more than what's outside. And luckily for us, most guys would rather be with a nice girl like Bella than with a bombshell with no brains and a bad attitude.

So hang in there, girls, because it's true: your guy's gonna love you mainly for who you are, not for what you look like.

But in terms of Hollywood hotties versus Rosalie, and even Alice, let's face it: these vampire goddesses could beat out any human girl, even Scarlett Johansson and Jennifer Lopez.

as somewhat different from the typical vampires seen in films. In most movies, the male vampire has dark, glowing eyes that often turn red when he's intoxicating his victims. He rarely has purplish bruises beneath his eyes, and he rarely looks exhausted. Unless you count the ancient look of the vampire in his pure batlike form, withered, gnarled, and looking like a bat corpse; there are no purplish bruises beneath the eyes because the entire face is one giant bruise!

Now, when Bella sits next to Edward in biology class on her first day, his eyes are so dark that they're black. Later in the novels, she thinks of his eyes as bronze. This is very much in line with the standard vampire look: black eyes when thirsty; and molten, mesmerizing, reddish bronze eyes when drinking blood or lusting for it.

Edward's voice is melodic, as are the voices of most vampires we encounter in films. Their voices are smooth, charming, their pronunciation of words is almost lyrical. And Bella finds Edward's

VAMPIRIC EYES

In most fiction and movies, the vampire's eyes shine with fierce intensity and are brilliant in color. Set in very pale skin, the vampire's eyes have a luminescent glow that attracts human attention.

In Anne Rice's Vampire Chronicles,[2] for example, the vampire Louis has vivid green, glowing eyes. Lestat's eyes are grayish, but they can absorb colors and turn into brilliant blues and violets. Talk about mesmerizing!

Bela Lugosi's eyes, as well as the eyes of Nosferatu, are extremely dark and turn red when the vampire is lusting for blood or finishing a long drink. This is similar to Edward, except Edward's eyes really don't turn red, rather, they become liquid bronze. Personally, I find a molten bronze look far more appealing than bright red eyes. The molten look is much sexier and more passionate.

2. Anne Rice's Vampire Chronicles is a series of novels beginning with *Interview with the Vampire*, which was published by Alfred A. Knopf in 1976.

Vampire eyes are traditionally hypnotic. In the original Dracula film, Bela Lugosi rises from his coffin, turns his head, and stares at poor Jonathan Harker, who is hoping to kill the vampire. Instead, Harker falls under the hypnotic spell of Dracula's eyes.

And we all know that, once a vampire bites a girl, she's forever under his spell. He can still use his eyes to make her do what he wants, but he can also just mentally call her from far away, and she'll rise as if a zombie, leave her bedroom, wander into the dark, misty night, and throw herself at the blood-sucking monster.

Before Bela Lugosi, depictions of vampires didn't necessarily show them with hypnotic, glowing eyes. Varney the Vampire from the 1800s[3] didn't hypnotize anyone, and neither did the female Carmilla,[4] who seduced men into letting her bite their necks.

But Bela Lugosi set a new high bar for all vampires that were to come after him. If you haven't seen the 1931 film, make sure to get a copy and watch it. Notice how Lugosi's eyes stare into the camera, hypnotizing not only his victims but also audiences for decades ever since.

---

3. Featured in *Varney the Vampire: or, The Feast of Blood* written by James Malcolm Rymer in the mid-1840s. Even back then, the vampire had pale skin, long fangs for sucking blood, long fingernails, and most important, shining eyes that were described as metallic.
4. Featured in the short story "Carmilla," written by Joseph Sheridan Le Fanu in 1872.

lips to be perfect and beautiful, as well, and while most vampires in film might have nice smiles, they generally have lips that aren't so perfect. Most vampire lips are either bloodless and thin, or smeared in red as if dipped in blood; it depends on how hungry they are, I suppose. But vampire lips, in general, aren't their best feature.

When a vampire touches a girl, she feels electricity, like a bolt of sexual attraction coursing through her. This is most definitely the case with Bella, because every time Edward touches her at all, she feels the intense voltage of physical attraction. This common vampire trait is something that vampires use to attract their victims. The eyes, the musical tones of their voices, the electric touch: all typical of vampires and all reasons why we find them so irresistible and sexy.

So there's definitely an allure of vampires for us mortal girls in that they basically hypnotize us. And female vampires seduce human men, luring them with great beauty and hypnotic stares until the men fall prey to their fangs.

As for being handsome, some standard vampires are charming and sauve, such as the original Count Dracula played by Bela Lugosi, and more current vampires such as Louis de Pointe du Lac, played by Brad Pitt, and Lestat de Lioncourt, played by Tom Cruise, in the 1994 film *Interview with the Vampire* directed by Neil Jordan. But some are repulsive, such as Nosferatu, played by the infamous Max Schreck in the original movie, and later by Willem Dafoe in the 2000 film *Shadow of the Vampire*. Another repulsive Dracula is played by Gary Oldman in the 1992 remake of Bram Stoker's Dracula film, conveniently titled *Bram Stoker's Dracula*. In the 1992 movie, Dracula is handsome, charming, and sauve when he wants to be, but he's totally repulsive and ancient at other times. In the case of Lugosi's Dracula, he was definitely a charmer, but he was also middle-aged and not at all like gorgeous, seventeen-year-old Edward; he wasn't shockingly handsome by the standards of today's teenagers, though he was a very attractive man for some-one who is middle-aged.

Naturally, vampire teeth are perfect and very white, unless the vampire has just consumed a large meal of blood. Vampires never seem to have cavities, rotting brown teeth, chipped or missing teeth. I often wonder: if a human who already has terrible teeth turns into a vampire, how do his rotting, brown, cavity-ridden teeth suddenly become so white and perfect? It's one of those vampire mysteries that has followed me throughout life.

Regardless, Edward, of course, has perfect teeth that are bril-liant white. And, as with all vampires, he has perfect teeth de-spite the fact that he died *a really long time ago* . . . long before humans had good dental care.

I think we've established that Edward is gorgeous, and certainly, Bella thinks so. In fact, remembering all the guys in my high school class, of which there were hundreds, I can't think of one guy who looked as good as Edward. Sure, we had some handsome dudes who were really popular—what school doesn't have them?—but, did they have Edward's butterscotch eyes, auburn hair, pale skin, per-fect smile, and electric touch? No way. (Not that I experienced the touches of any of those perfect guys in my high school!)

Most vampires are handsome in their own way, but all of them are superstrong. By superstrong, I mean: they have the muscles and speed of superheroes. They can fly and run so fast you don't see them. They can grip a man so tightly, he's simply crushed. In Edward's case, he not only runs about as fast as the speed of light, he can lift cars and does so to save Bella's life. And Bella describes him frequently as if he is a blend of a superhero and a god.

Can you imagine this guy on the track team?

Or lifting weights in a gym? He could be Mr. Olympia like Arnold Schwarzenegger, who won the Mr. Olympia bodybuilding world title seven times. In fact, though Arnold was known as the World's Strongest Man by 1970, there's no way he could have defeated Edward Cullen.

Lots of girls go for guys who are handsome and strong, though most girls have enough sense to want a dude who has intelligence and a nice personality, too. Personally, I don't care if my man can lift a truck if he's a moron with no brains or personality. Of course, if Conan the Barbarian showed up, I might have a hard time turning him down. Played famously by Arnold Schwarzenegger, Conan the Barbarian was the creation of Robert E. Howard in 1932. Conan originally appeared in many stories in a magazine called *Weird Tales*. I've read many Conan books and comics, and Arnold's Conan movies, camp as they are, rank among my favorite films.

Of course, unlike many vampires, Edward is extremely nice with basically a perfect personality. He's kind, compassionate, loving, adoring, and faithful. Like all vampires, he's extremely intelligent.

All of this sums up to a very sexy guy, who just happens to be an immortal vampire.

Given his immortality, a girl doesn't have to worry that her man might die in a world war, or fall down a pit or off a cliff, and leave her forever. In fact, she's going to be *stuck* with him forever. Literally, *forever*. He's never going to leave her, because vampire guys are in love with their girls for eternity. With the divorce rate hovering at about 50 percent, let's hope Bella and Edward *really* get along well. Even mortals, who might be married for ten, twenty, or fifty years, often have hard times, but imagine being married until the *end of all time*.

So Edward sucks blood. So he lives on blood. So he kills people.

No wait, unlike vampires in most stories, Edward doesn't kill people, does he? Edward confines himself to animals in the woods. He never kills any humans, and he never hurts their pets. He's a good vampire, with a soul.

He's beautiful, strong, and immortal, loving Bella forever: hey, what's *not* to like?

CHAPTER 3

WHAT TO EXPECT WHEN
YOU FALL IN LOVE WITH A VAMPIRE

✧

All girls fall in love at some point in life. In fact, some of us fall in love more than once. But our first love is memorable, and we never forget our first kiss and our first true romance. This happens for guys, too, or so I'm told.

But imagine if your first love happens to be a vampire, like Edward Cullen. Your first kiss could lead to a bite in the neck. At minimum, the kiss will send you reeling into a dizzy frenzy of excitement.

The entire notion of vampirism is hooked to erotic and romantic ideals. It's hooked into the dark, the night, the time when people meet, party, find romance, and seek love. It's hooked into dark adventure, living on the edge of pain. And it's hooked into the desire of the unknown and forbidden.

Take Bella, for example. Her boyfriend, Edward, is clearly forbidden, and she keeps her relationship with Edward a secret from her father for as long as possible. Bella knows that her father won't approve of Edward Cullen.

And, in addition to being forbidden, he's certainly an unknown. For a very long time, she knows little about him, and though she keeps asking him questions, he doesn't supply many answers along the way. Part of his allure is that she doesn't know much about him. He's a mystery man.

As for dark adventure and living on the edge of pain, Bella can have her fill of both by hooking up with Edward. Adventures with Edward include near death at the hands of the vampire James (played by Cam Gigandet in the Twilight movie), resulting in four broken ribs, cracks in her skull, a broken leg, and bruises all over her entire body. Most girls wouldn't be enticed to endure this kind of suffering to stay with a high school boyfriend. Most girls would be persuaded by family and friends to find a new guy who doesn't put her in so much danger. James actually bites Bella, infecting her with his "venom," but she survives because Edward is able to suck the venom out of her blood. After coming this close to death, how many girls would remain with their boyfriends?

Then there's Laurent, who attacks her after James is destroyed by the Cullen family. Laurent's eyes are red, not golden like the good vampires, and his objective is to kill Bella. Had I been attacked by and almost killed by so many "people" connected to my high school boyfriend, my father would have locked me in the house every night. Luckily, Bella is protected by the mental telepathy instructions sent by Edward. And luckily, gigantic werewolves show up to save the day. For most of us, if we said that mental telepathy and werewolves were saving our lives, people would think that we were completely out of our minds.

Bella's absorption in the Cullen clan threatens not only her, but also her new vampire family as well as her human parents. The dark adventures threaten the existence of the Cullen family, which has to hide amidst humans and never be exposed. In a small town such as where I live, near deaths caused by vampire and werewolf clashes would definitely be noticed. There is just so much that a hood of gray clouds can cover. As they fight James and Laurent, not to mention Jacob and the other werewolves, it becomes riskier for the Cullens—and for Bella's beloved Edward—to remain in Forks. Bella's parents, Charlie and Renée, are also at risk. James actually stalks her mother in hopes of luring and killing Bella, and as real girls would do, the fictional Bella fears for her mother's safety and tries to help.

Bella is closer to the border between life and death, love and pain, than most girls her age will ever be. She hovers between humanity and vampirism, she hovers between her love for Edward and near-death experiences and excruciating pain. Her love is as excruciating as it gets, and nothing—not soap operas, not romance novels, not steamy films—can come close to her experiences with Edward. While teenage first loves are usually incredibly emotional, fictional first loves transcend anything we feel in real life.

Despite the pain and near-death experiences, Bella can't resist Edward and everything for which he stands. The dark adventures are worth every minute of love with Edward. Many real girls remain deeply devoted and in love with their first loves even if their adventures become risky or dark. Yet for Bella, even when Edward ditches her for many months, her heart remains faithful, and this aspect is hard to imagine for a real girl. As fans, we might want to believe with all our hearts that our love would be this strong, that even if our soul-mate boyfriend ditched us seemingly forever, we would remain faithful and consumed with our love for him. In reality, this would be very hard to do for the simple fact that he has willingly left us forever.

So if you fall in love with a vampire, don't expect a simple, comfortable life. If you have any desire to scale corporate ladders, Edward is probably not the best choice for your man. After many years, it will become increasingly difficult to tell your boss and coworkers why your man never eats or drinks, why he won't go swimming at the beach or to various mundane office parties.

Of course, who wants to climb corporate ladders? Personally, I'd much rather have love. This makes me (and possibly you) different from feminist women who desire primarily to achieve their career goals. I've been grown up for a long time and have children of my own, and I've met plenty of career-driven women. Other than writing books such as this one, I have also worked for many years in companies and at universities. So it's not as if I have no career and I'm simply consumed by some ditzy love-type haze. Being a single mother, I recognize the need to support oneself and one's children. But still, my love for my children is much greater than any career option that might present itself.

At any rate, other than a corporate job, let's suppose that you choose a career path that leads to being a professor at a university. There are department parties and other social events, where your man must make an appearance. Once again, how do you explain to your coworkers that your man cannot go with you on that free conference trip to the beach, that he won't eat or drink anything? If you become a tenured faculty member, you'll know and work with the same group of people for the rest of your life; and all of them will get to know your man, Edward. It will be incredibly hard to hide the fact that he's not human, that he's a vampire.

But who cares, right? These minor problems can be worked out. Many professions don't require that your man ever mingle with your boss or coworkers.

However, just don't work in a blood bank.

If you fall in love with a vampire, you also might consider

Bella's approach, whereby she wants Edward to transform her into a vampire, too. Would you really want to be married to a man who remains seventeen forever while you turn thirty, forty, sixty, ninety? It's gross just to think about it. So either your man has to become mortal again, or he has to bite your neck, suck your blood, and turn you into a vampire.

If your Edward becomes mortal again, he might hold it against you someday. Suppose the two of you break up. He's all

BEAUTY AND THE VAMPIRE

As you age and your Edward remains seventeen, you're going to have to take really good care of your looks. When you're thirty and he's still seventeen, you have to look twenty, or at worst, twenty-two years old. This is going to be hard to do as the years slide by.

In addition, you'll want to hide the fact that there's blood in your body. This means maintaining a pallor on your face, hiding any blushes or rosy cheeks. It would also help to have purple bruises or, at minimum, deep, dark circles, beneath your eyes. With contact lenses, you might be able to have molten golden eyes. The key is to fit into the vampire world you intend to live in for the rest of your life. Why should you go to such extremes to look like a vampire? You choose the reasons:

A. You intend to hang out with vampires for decades. It might be wise to disguise the fact that you're human, that is, *food*. Sure, the vampires will still sense that you have blood in your body, but it's wise to hide your blood as best as you can. You never know if your Edward has a hostile cousin, an Anne Rice–style Laurent, or an ancient Roman vampire who doesn't understand the etiquette of not feasting on Edward's wife.

B. The Goth look is cool. Who wouldn't want to look like a cadaver at all times?

C. If you already look dead, nobody will try to kill you. You will be able to walk down the streets of the worst city on the planet, and nobody will attack you.

D. Why tempt your Edward to suck your blood? It's so hard for him to resist killing you, as it is, so why tempt fate? It's better to look pale, drained of blood, and unappetizing.

The correct answers are A and D, and if you like the Goth look, then you can add B to the list. But C is incorrect. Even if you look dead, as long as you're staggering around a dark, dangerous city at two A.M., you're asking for trouble. Most killers won't assume you're a zombie or other form of walking dead; they'll assume you're still alive no matter how bad you look.

It'll cost a bit to maintain the look of the dead. For example, you need an ample supply of SPF 50 (or more) sunscreen to protect your entire body, especially your face, from any form of blush or bronze glow. A suntan is out of the question. A sunburn is asking for Edward or one of his pals to drain the blood out of your body. It's like walking around in front of a normal flesh-and-blood seventeen-year-old boy in nothing but fishnet stockings and a thong—you're asking for trouble with your vampire man if you come home with blistered, sunburned skin. So buy a *case* of SPF 50.

(continued)

With your golden contact lenses in place, you now want to apply a liberal amount of blue-black or purplish blue shadow under both eyes. Use a waterproof cream, if you can find it. It's a dead (sorry) giveaway if your vampiric deep, dark circles start running from your eyes down your face.

To make your golden eyes really stand out, apply heavy amounts of black liner around both eyes. Heavy black mascara might help, too. Make sure all cosmetics are waterproof.

At this point, you're about three hours into your daily beauty regimen, and this is, as noted, just to make sure none of your vampire friends and family accidentally kills you.

Always have on hand a bulk supply of waterproof, theatrical, cream-based white foundation. Smear it liberally all over your face and body, from your hairline to the tips of your toes. Make sure to coat your ears. You might want to leave a little breathing room for your skin. Choose areas on your body where most people won't notice that you have ordinary skin tones. The inner belly button might work, for example, or the crack in your rear (sorry, but that is a good place to avoid smearing heavy white cosmetics). The souls of your feet can remain unsmeared—just keep your shoes on at all times. And if you intend to remain fully clothed all day, you can leave all clothed sections of your body free of the vampiric influence.

Black or bright red lipstick completes the vampiric facial look. Try to buy the type that doesn't rub off, even if you're drinking water. Real vampires like Edward do not have lips that rub off; their lips are blackish if they're thirsty for blood, and reddish if they've just feasted. Your lips should look as similar as possible.

As for clothes, don't go with the Goth look because Edward

and his family don't look like Goths. Wear ordinary clothes as they do. Don't give any vampire the idea that you're trying too hard to fit in. Instead, you'll stick out as an obvious human.

Perhaps an exception is your swimsuit selection. If you go to the beach, try to wear a one-piece suit, the type your grandma might wear, so most of your body is covered. Always wear sunglasses and a big hat to the beach, also like Grandma. I would also recommend a long-sleeved shirt and pants, just for extra protection from the sun. A dark rashguard protects you best from the sun's rays, and you can obtain matching spandex black pants to pull over your bathing suit. Avoid the sun, any blushing, any tanning, and certainly, any burning at all costs.

As you become more experienced with the daily six-hour beauty preparation, try dabbing a little blue on your lips and face for that extra-drained look. A light wash of blue tint is best.

Finally, to truly fit in with your new family and friends, learn to move as gracefully as possible. Your steps should be quick, with your goal to be moving so fast people can't see you. Yes, I know it's impossible, but if you work toward this goal, you might be able to teach yourself how to move very quickly without falling over chairs, accidentally tripping old ladies, and crashing into doors.

alone. What other woman will ever even *believe* that he was once a vampire? Nobody will ever know his true self, and his loneliness could lead to depression, and even worse. He could end up really hating you. Had he remained a vampire, at least he could have had his "other" family to keep him company forever.

And his youth and good looks to charm women. If you make your vampire man become mortal again somehow, just make sure you hold on to him and never let go.

In a similar manner, if he turns you into a vampire, as Bella wishes Edward would do, make really sure you love this guy enough to stay with him for, say, a thousand years. I'm not sure how a judge would handle a divorce when the couple's been together for a thousand years, or even two hundred years. Maybe there's a cap on how long people can be married, like two hundred years, and then the marriage is considered null and void anyway. But regardless, with both of you being immortal vampires, you're bound to cross paths more than once during a thousand years, even if you break up. So make your marriage choice carefully.

Also, keep in mind that, even if your guy is sucking the necks of lots of other women, he really loves you and only you. So don't get too jealous if your man starts creeping around in the dead of night to hang out in beautiful women's bedrooms and nuzzle them. It's their blood he wants, that's all. I can't imagine Edward sucking the blood of any girl other than Bella, but in a thousand-year relationship, who knows what will happen? After all, he's a guy, and a thousand years is a long time to spend with just one woman.

One thing is clear. If you fall in love with a vampire, don't expect your parents to be happy. They will want cute, human grandchildren. They'll think twice before babysitting your vampire baby. Then there's snack time. Most grandmothers like to supply their toddler grandchildren with cookies and milk, or at least that's what all the urban myths tell us. If your baby is at all vampiric, will your mother really enjoy giving him cookies and a cup of blood? Probably not.

On the upside, your engagement ring will probably be many hundreds of years old and really cool looking. Your guy will have the manners of world-class gentlemen from times long past. He'll adore you and treat you very well, and you will be intoxicated by your love for him. And if you have a taste for living in an ancient castle in a remote place, all of your wishes might come true.

CHAPTER 4

BELLA'S AWAKENING:
What Really Happens When You Turn into a Vampire

✧

Many people dream about becoming a vampire, which is why the entire subject of vampirism is probably so popular. There's something very romantic and appealing about the vampire, as we discussed a bit in the last few chapters.

For one thing, if you are "lucky" enough to turn into a vampire, you can live forever. For another, you suddenly possess super-human strength, as when Edward Cullen saves Bella Swan by grabbing and holding a van before it can crush her. And even more, you suddenly become radiantly beautiful or handsome, depending on your gender. If you're a girl, expect to be so gorgeous that a mere sideways glance from you will turn any man of any age into a slobbering, doting slave to your every desire. You won't have to worry about diets anymore, because you'll live on blood and remain thin and young forever.

BELLA AND ACCIDENTS

Bella Swan doesn't like to play sports because she's always tripping, falling, and hurting herself. She just seems to beg for accidents to happen to her. Poor Edward Cullen is always worrying about Bella, keeping her in sight (or in mind through telepathy when they're apart). He constantly has to save her from attacks and accidents.

Bella is what some people call "accident prone." Scientists, who study everything from claustrophobia in elevators to toenail ripples, have tried to determine what makes some people more accident prone than others.

For example, the February 2006 issue of *Occupational Medicine*[1] reported the findings of a French team of researchers who studied 2,610 French railway workers and found that 27 percent of the workers had far more accidents than the others. Reasons cited for being highly accident prone were what you might imagine: exhaustion, job inexperience, lack of exercise, bad attitude about the job, and so forth. And the reasons cited for not being accident prone were also what you might guess: that you learn from others and from past experiences, that you are conscientious, and that you are an easygoing sort of person.

No huge surprises here, but none of these factors about being highly accident prone tends to pertain to Bella Swan. She's not particularly exhausted, she's more than experienced at her studies (actually having learned most of it before moving to Forks), she has plenty of exercise (running from vampire killers), and she has a good attitude about things, in general.

In May 2007, *New Scientist* analyzed findings from a

1. Reported by Dr. Stephen Juan in *The Register*, October 2006, at http://www.theregister.co.uk/2006/10/20/the_odd_body_accident_proneness.

(continued)

report[2] made by the University Medical Center Groningen in the Netherlands. The report is drawn from data collected in seventy-nine studies about 147,000 accident-prone people in fifteen countries. The authors of the report conclude that one in twenty-nine people have a 50 percent higher chance of tripping, falling, hurting themselves, or otherwise having accidents than the rest of us.

But as with the earlier 2006 study, the reasons why some people are incredibly accident prone remain unknown. The 2007 report concludes that these people are just "hapless."

Hapless means "unfortunate," so the conclusion is accurate, we'll give them that much! If you trip over a rug at least once a day and bonk your head on a metal table, you're an unfortunate, or hapless, person. If you blow up the kitchen trying to cook eggs, you're more than unfortunate. If you're mowing the lawn and accidentally mow off all of your toes, I'd say you're way beyond hapless.

So what is it about Bella Swan that makes her so accident prone? Perhaps we'll find the answers in the fourth book of the Twilight Saga.

---

2. "Accident-prone people do exist," *New Scientist*, May 16, 2007, at http://www.newscientist.com/article.ns?id=mg19426034.600.

The downside, of course, is that you *will* have to live on blood for the rest of your eternal life. Although, it's possible you may be able to get away with drinking animal blood and eating insects rather than draining the blood out of the necks of your best friends. This will require enormous self-control, so if you don't have much self-control now, it might be best not to assume that you will be able to survive forever without a drop of human blood.

Bella Swan's best friend, werewolf Jacob Black of the Quileute Indian Tribe, points out that Edward and the Cullen family do have that level of self-control, that they don't attack humans for their blood, that they do subsist instead on animal blood. Bella, of course, learns this fact for herself, and doesn't seem terribly perturbed that her boyfriend and his family hunt for bears and other wildlife at night in order to suck up animal blood.

QUILEUTE INDIAN TRIBE

As for the Quileute Indian Tribe, it is a real Indian tribe in the area of Forks, Washington. The Quileutes have been settled there for as long as they can remember, harking back to "thousands of winters before the arrival of the White Drifting-House people . . ."[3] It is said that the tribe began during the Ice Age. The Web site for the tribe states that the real Quileutes have a story about their origin that is directly tied to wolves. A "wandering Transformer" changed all of the Indians from wolves. They fished, hunted, and made blankets from the fur of their dogs. Because the rainfall often reaches fifteen inches in a season, the Indians made rainproof clothes from soft cedar bark.[4]

The Quileute tribe consists of less than a thousand people, most of them in La Push, Washington.

---

3. http://www.quileutenation.org/index.cfm?page=history.html.
4. Ibid.

Still, gnawing on the neck of a bear and draining its body of fluids beats the alternate diet of human blood. Edward has the self-control of a saint. As with religion, we can assume that you can be an orthodox vampire (attack people, drink human blood daily), a conservative vampire (bite people's necks in their sleep, drink human blood when you're really hungry), or a reformed vampire (never attack people, drink only animal blood). The Cullen family is clearly reformed.

Bella longs to become a vampire so she can live forever with Edward, both of them remaining in their teens. She cannot stand the thought of being an old lady with a seventeen-year-old Edward, and frankly, I don't blame her. But what is she *really* asking him to do?

Whatever it is, Edward absolutely refuses, from *Twilight* to *New Moon* to *Eclipse*. Fans eagerly waited for August 2, 2008, when Stephenie Meyer revealed these and other secrets in the fourth book of the series, *Breaking Dawn*. As soon as the fourth book was in stores, I bought a copy and read it immediately, as I began writing this book when only the first three books in the series were available.

Women often go through many hours, sometimes a day or more, of labor to give birth. And for many women, labor is extremely painful. In approximately the eighteenth hour of heavy labor prior to the birth of my son, I was howling in agony and begging my doctor to "just hit me over the head with a hammer and get it over with."

Does a vampire transformation require this level of torment?

According to the Twilight Saga, it does, and then some: when a vampire bites the neck of a person, venom is released into the victim's blood. It takes days for the victim to turn into a vampire, and those days are filled with excruciating pain and agony.

It is when the heart stops beating that the victim is a true vampire.

Frankly, after giving birth, turning into a vampire doesn't sound all that difficult. So if someone, say Bella, knowing all the risks, wants to be a vampire badly enough, she can probably suffer through a few days of hell to get there.

In movies and books, there are many types of vampires. Some, like the Cullen clan, are born by the method just described. Some are already corpses that are reanimated, some are spirits that invade host bodies and take them over in a vampiric manner. But let's explore, for now, the Cullen form of transformation into a vampire.

First, when someone actually dies—that is, dies and does not turn into a vampire—his heart stops beating, and due to gravity, the remaining blood in the body moves toward the ground. So if the dead person is on his back, the blood will shift into the regions of the back of his legs, the back of his arms, and the back of his torso, and so forth. Due to the lack of red blood cells, the corpse's body turns waxy and pale.

Now, I don't want to gross you out, and to be honest, while it's disgusting to read about human decomposition, it's even more disgusting to write about it. But to understand the state of the dead, and subsequently the undead such as the vampire, requires some rudimentary knowledge. I will be as delicate as possible, mainly because it's approximately noon and I'm hungry, and I'd rather not even attempt to eat lunch while writing about human decomposition.

With a grape in my mouth, I will continue. This will keep you, my dear readers, from any chance that the text will hereby get really gross.

After approximately ten to twelve hours of the pale and waxy look, which is vampirish, the dead human body starts turning into odd shades of pink, purple, and blue. So if a current vampire transforms you within, say, ten hours, you might end up waxy and pale forever rather than pink, purple, and blue.

This blotching of the skin is due to something called livor mortis, or deoxygenation. Eventually, the color will become quite dark, like a giant bruise covering the entire body.

I'm popping another grape into my mouth and bypassing any explanation of insect infestation of the corpse.

After deoxygenation, the corpse's arms and legs turn blue, and the body temperature plummets at the rate of about two degrees per hour. Finally, rigor mortis sets in, which I'm sure you've all heard about on countless television and movie crime dramas. Rigor mortis means that the corpse stiffens into a rigid boardlike state. In the end, of course, the body decomposes, but for our purposes, we can skip that part. Suffice it to say that the lips curl back, the eyes protrude, and the external skin peels and exposes new skin beneath.

Now, if this poor sap, our dead guy in the above example, happens to get lucky and be bitten by a vampire right before death, he might go through a few days of agony, but at least he won't turn blue-black, bloat, burst, and ooze. In fact, he might end up with waxy, pale skin along with thin, reddish blue, evil-looking lips, and protruding eyes. Reminds you of the standard vampire, doesn't it?

I'm not sure how the new vampire goes from looking literally like a corpse into looking like a glam queen, but perhaps the venom suggested by Edward Cullen is a youth serum.

During the three days of torment following the vampiric bite, the victim typically shows signs of extreme illness, such as those seen when somebody has tuberculosis. The symptoms of tuberculosis include chest pains, difficulty in breathing, coughing up blood, exhaustion, fever, weakness, loss of appetite, loss of weight, and pale skin. Someone with tuberculosis will have a hard time making it through the night, will appear to be wasting away, and will rasp when trying to breathe. In short, she will behave like anyone bitten by a vampire in most movies and books.

The word *nosferatu* is derived from the Greek word *nosophoros*, which means "plague carrier." Long ago, people believed that vampires carried the plague, specifically a disease such as tuberculosis. In those days, the cause of tuberculosis was unknown, so figuring it was spread by the bites of vampires made sense to people.

It's possible that Edward's venom serves not only to preserve the victim's beauty, but also to make the actual transformation due to some form of genetic mechanism. Venom is basically a toxin. Venom is injected in the animal community using stings, bristles, and of course, fangs. Some venoms can kill instantly just with one drop. Among mammals, venomous varieties include the male platypus and shrews.

Snake venoms, in particular, contain peptide toxins, which mean that the toxins are formed from polymers of linked amino acids. Sound familiar? You might remember from biology class that amino acids and peptide bonds are part of the genetic codes of animals.

Also of interest, some peptides act as hormones or enzymes, such as ribosomal peptides, which are synthesized during messenger RNA translation. And peptides are released by human cells into the blood, where they can then signal other activities in the body.

If Edward's venom is like that of snakes, it not only contains peptide toxins, but it causes pain, convulsions, and low blood pressure in the victim. So someone, such as Bella Swan, who wants to be transformed into a vampire, will indeed undergo pain, convulsions, and a drop in blood pressure after the big bite.

You might recall that the human genome contains many thousands of genes. But did you know that not all of the genes are active all the time? In fact, genes tend to switch on and off, as needed, and when a gene switches on, we say that it has been *expressed*. So, for example, when being transcribed into messenger RNA, the very process that synthesizes ribosomal peptides, genes are expressed.

In short, the vampire's venom acts as a virus of sorts, and it contains genetic material that it injects into the victim's cells. Inside the cells, the RNA interprets the genetic commands of the viral venom and then the ribosomes create additional venom enzymes. These new venom enzymes are viral in nature, meaning they attack other cells and inject their own DNA into them. And hence, the venom spreads throughout the body.

The venom causes a form of genetic mutation and makes sure the body's immune system does not flush out the virus. The newly formed vampire, say Bella, is transformed into one that feeds on blood, heals very quickly, is highly resistant to pain and harm, and so forth. In fact, the viral venom may also manipulate the genes that create pallor, hence making the vampire look pale and waxy.

We do know, just from reading the newspapers, that genetic engineering is advancing rapidly today. We're able to cut DNA from one cell and put it into the cell of another animal, and that second animal's cell will start manufacturing its own types of proteins. The protein sequences are determined by the genes, or DNA segments introduced into the second animal.

One common example of genetic engineering is synthetic human insulin. Another is human growth hormone, which apparently, many famous sports figures have been caught using. Today, we have genetically modified organisms such as fruits and vegetables that do not need pesticides to thrive well. We have knockout experiments, in which scientists remove genes from animals. We have experiments that induce the active synthesis of specific proteins.

If humans can do all of the above, then it's not a stretch to think that vampiric viral venom can kick up a genetic change in a victim and turn that victim into another vampire.

MERCY BROWN, THE EXETER VAMPIRE

In 1892 in Exeter, Rhode Island, a nineteen-year-old girl named Mercy Brown died of tuberculosis. Her father assumed she had contracted the disease from a vampiric undead family member, who had visited her at night and bit her. Mercy's mother, Mary, had already died of tuberculosis, and then her sister Mary Olive died from the disease. Soon after, Mercy's brother Edwin contracted tuberculosis, as well.

Townspeople and even the members of Mercy's family believed that one of the dead Browns had turned into what we would now call a vampire. Mercy's father, George, with the help of the villagers, exhumed her mother and sister. Then they opened the crypt of Mercy, who had been buried for two months above ground in freezing weather. While the first two bodies had decomposed considerably, Mercy's body still contained blood in the heart and still appeared human. Horrified,

(continued)

everyone thought that Mercy had turned into a vampire. What's more, everyone assumed that Mercy had infected her brother, Edwin, with the vampiric disease. It did not occur to George Brown or his family and friends that his wife and oldest daughter had died a long time ago, and hence, their bodies had decomposed, whereas Mercy had died recently during freezing weather. Instead, vampirism was the cause of her death, and her father, with the help of others, cut out her heart and burned it.

Even more grotesque, George Brown forced his dying son, Edwin, to drink a potion containing the burned heart ashes in hopes of avoiding a vampiric fate. Why George Brown thought this would work is questionable. Perhaps he was just a desperate man, having lost several family members already. Regardless, Edwin died a couple of months after drinking George's antivampire elixir.

CHAPTER 5

VAMPIRE QUIZ!

✧

Bella longs to be a vampire. So do you. Or, let's assume you do for the purposes of this chapter. Let's say you wake up tomorrow, and you are no longer just human. Instead, you look in the mirror and find that your eyes glow with an intensity known only to movie stars; that your skin is more pale than the pages of this book; that you have superstrength, super-glamour, and eternal life. And, of course, that you have an insatiable thirst for blood.

What kind of vampire would you be? A wild one, a sweet one, a violent one? Take this quiz and find out. Answer each question, then find out what kind of vampire you'd be at the end of the quiz.

Question #1. What kind of sheets are in your coffin (or bed, if you're like a Cullen vampire)?

   A. Black silk sheets
   B. High-quality ten-trillion-thread-count cotton sheets
   C. Blood-stained sheets
   D. The most beautiful and romantic sheets in the world
   E. You don't use sheets; instead, you use a blanket made of wolf fur

Question #2. You are a newly made vampire. All you want is human blood. You can't control the urge. Who do you drain first?

A. Your best friend

B. The school bully

C. The boy you liked who made fun of you, called you a fat slob and a dog, and rejected you in front of everyone

D. Your gym teacher because he makes you sweat too much

E. Your math teacher because you never know what he's talking about

F. One of the guys on *People* magazine's Top 10 Sexy Guys list, if you can get close enough to him

Question #3. You have drained someone of blood (see Question #2). It's already midnight. Most likely, there's a full moon out, and although you're not a dog (contrary to what that creepy kid said about you, see Question #2C), you feel like howling at the moon and raising hell. Where do you go to release all of that excess energy?

A. To a heavy-metal night club, where people are screaming and dancing in the dark while neon lights throb overhead

B. To a cemetery to dig up all the graves and gloat that *they* are all dead while *you* are now immortal

C. To your bedroom (or coffin) to catch up on all that homework and studying you've been neglecting since being gripped in the feverish torment of vampiric transformation

D. To a deserted, huge park where you can race around on a motorcycle at two hundred miles per hour and run in circles near the speed of light

Question #4. After calming down from your night of feasting and carousing, you take a long walk to kill time before the sun rises.

Up ahead is a castle with a gatepost with a crest and your name on it. Yes, you have found your vampiric castle. You are Duchess Veronique Van Cullen with vast new treasures. You enter the castle. What is the first thing that captures your attention?

A. The stairs leading to the basement where you know you'll find the damp, the musk, the dark earth, and the coffins

B. The fine oil painting of the first Duchess Veronique Van Cullen, who "died" in 1232. You wonder where she is now.

C. The ankle-length, black-and-pink silk-and-lace gown that is custom made just for your body (and that of the first Duchess Veronique Van Cullen, whose measurements were 37–22–34). You are thrilled that your body is now so glamorous! With this gown, you are sure to attract any mortal male you want.

D. The black leather miniskirt with matching corset that makes you look even better than you do in the gown (see C, above). You try on the outfit. With the spiked black heels that you find beneath the oil painting, you look like a vamp sure to catch the guys.

E. An oil painting of the first Duke François Van Cullen, who is so handsome you almost faint. If you look like the first duchess, you know that there's a guy out there, just waiting for you, who looks like the first duke.

Question #5. What are you most afraid of now that you're a vampire?

A. Werewolves

B. The sun

C. Living forever all alone without Duke François Van Cullen

D. Sleeping in coffins

E. Having to hunt for prey

Question #6. You wander through your castle, kicking rats aside and swiping cobwebs off your face. You come to a Victorian bedroom with a big, four-post bed and an adjoined study. Someone has recently slept in the bed, you notice. Curious, you enter the study, where you see two thrones, and in one of the thrones is Duke François Van Cullen! What does he look like?

    A. He looks like Edward Cullen.

    B. He is six foot ten inches tall, has gladiator muscles, a huge smile with pearly white teeth, glowing blue eyes, and black hair.

    C. He is five foot two inches tall, has a concave chest and no muscles, a thin smile with pointed teeth, beady black eyes, and gray hair.

    D. He is five foot ten inches tall, weighs 340 pounds, and as you enter the room, he's stuffing four entire chickens into his mouth.

Question #7. What do you say to your true love when you see him for the first time?

    A. Come on over here, sailor boy! Mama's got a treat for you.

    B. You can't talk. You just stand there, blushing and shivering.

    C. Hey, nice seeing you, Duke ol' boy, are you a vampire, too?

    D. Are you for real?

Question #8. He says that he has waited for you and only you for well over seven hundred years. He has never fallen in love. Not since his beloved duchess died from consumption. How do you respond?

    A. Come on over here, sailor boy! Mama's got a treat for you.

    B. You can't talk. You just stand there, blushing and shivering.

    C. You tell him that you suspect that the two of you have a lot in common, both being vampires, and that you'd like to hang out with him—as much as possible. Then you swoon and faint.

D. You have got to be kidding. What kind of fool do you take me for?

Question #9. There's a mirror across the throne room. You know better than to go near it. Do you think that you're going to miss seeing yourself in the mirror?

A. Yes. You are *that* vain.

B. No. Besides, you'd rather look at the duke.

Question #10. Would you mind turning into a wolf, a bat, and mist from time to time?

A. The wolf and bat: I wouldn't like that at all.

B. Turning into mist would be kind of cool. I could roil down the school halls and creep people out when I'm in the city. It might be fun to be a huge mist rolling into math class one day and filling up the room. I could handle the wolf form when I need to save someone or command the pack, and I think I could handle the bat form for fast transportation in a pinch.

C. I would mind all of it. I don't want to be a wolf, a bat, or mist.

D. I'm beginning to wonder if I can transform back from vampire into pure human again.

That's it, you've answered all ten questions. And now it's time to find out what kind of vampire you would be if you woke up one morning and found out you had transformed. Let's go through the questions one at a time:

ANSWERS

Question #1. What kind of sheets are in your coffin (or bed, if you're like a Cullen vampire)?

A. Black silk sheets

B. High-quality ten-trillion-thread-count cotton sheets

C. Blood-stained sheets

D. The most beautiful and romantic sheets in the world

E. You don't use sheets; instead, you use a blanket made of wolf fur

If you chose A, black silk sheets, you're probably not Edward's type of girl. While black silk sheets may be exotic and sexy, they're not the kind of sheets a vampire girl would sleep in if she were trying to fit in with normal humans. I mean, come on: how many of *your* friends have black silk sheets?

If you chose B, high-quality ten-trillion-thread-count cotton sheets, you'd make a good vampire girl in a very rich neighborhood. Nobody would ever suspect you of being a vampire. But if you're not rich, then this would be a poor choice because you'd really stand out and everyone would watch you constantly.

If you chose C, blood-stained sheets, you are definitely a vampire. But again, all of your friends are going to be awfully suspicious!

If you chose D, the most beautiful and romantic sheets in the world, you are probably the kind of girl that Edward would like. Nobody will ever suspect you of being a vampire, which is exactly what you want. This answer is pretty boring, but I'd choose it if it meant I had a chance with a guy like Edward.

Finally, if you chose E, a blanket made of wolf fur, you're asking for trouble. You are a feisty vampire girl, full of spirit. I'd probably like you because you sound like fun, but you're gonna get in a lot of trouble with all of those werewolves in town.

Question #2. You are a newly made vampire. All you want is human blood. You can't control the urge. Who do you drain first?

   A. Your best friend

   B. The school bully

   C. The boy you liked, who made fun of you, called you a fat slob and a dog, and rejected you in front of everyone

   D. Your gym teacher because he makes you sweat too much

   E. Your math teacher because you never know what he's talking about

   F. One of the guys on *People* magazine's Top 10 Sexy Guys list, if you can get close enough to him

I hope you did not choose A, your best friend. If so, shame on you! Your best friend should be the last person you'd drain of blood.

If you chose B, the school bully, I'd say you're doing all your human friends a big favor. After all, you're a vampire and you've gotta eat—I mean, drink—and why not choose a disgusting guy like the school bully instead of someone nice?

If you chose C, the boy who called you a fat slob and a dog, and rejected you in front of everyone, think carefully about your answer. Are you sure you want your Edward to think of you as a vindictive loser? Wouldn't it make more sense to take the high road, ignore the boy in question whenever you pass him, and be happy to be seen with your new, perfectly handsome vampire boyfriend?

If you chose D or E, your gym or math teacher, let me know right away so I make sure never to become a teacher. Not that I am at all physically equipped to be a gym teacher, and not that I am at all mentally equipped to be a math teacher. But I want to know, just in case I decide to teach writing classes at a high school somewhere.

Finally, if you selected F, one of those top ten sexy guys, I'm right with you, babe! If you have to be a vampire and have to nibble on some guy's neck, let it be one of the top ten most sexy guys on the planet.

Question #3. You have drained someone of blood (see Question #2). It's already midnight. Most likely, there's a full moon out, and although you're not a dog (contrary to what that creepy kid said about you, see Question #2C), you feel like howling at the moon and raising hell. Where do you go to release all of that excess energy?

    A. To a heavy-metal night club, where people are screaming and dancing in the dark while neon lights throb overhead

    B. To a cemetery to dig up all the graves and gloat that *they* are all dead while *you* are now immortal

    C. To your bedroom (or coffin) to catch up on all that homework and studying you've been neglecting since being gripped in the feverish torment of vampiric transformation

    D. To a deserted, huge park where you can race around on a motorcycle at two hundred miles per hour and run in circles near the speed of light

If you chose A, to a heavy-metal night club, where people are screaming and dancing in the dark while neon lights throb overhead, you are a typical vampire. Very good choice! After my first night of feasting as a vampire and getting all psyched up, I'd probably want to scream and dance in a dark club all night, too.

If you chose B, to a cemetery to dig up all the graves and gloat that *they* are all dead while *you* are now immortal, then you are showing your vindictive side. Not a good trait, even for a vampire.

As for C, to your bedroom to catch up on all the homework and studying you've missed while transforming into a vampire, you're admirable but being pretty silly. Sweetheart, you are going to live for hundreds of years, maybe thousands. You will remain seventeen (or whatever your current age) for the rest of eternity. This means, to fit into human communities such as Forks, you will have to take the same year of high school classes for a very long time, over and over again. Having just turned into a vampire, now is not the time to catch up on trigonometry. Do it tomorrow.

As for answer D, to a deserted, huge park where you can race around on a motorcycle at two hundred miles per hour and run in circles near the speed of light, this is a very good answer, just like answer A was an excellent choice. However, dancing in a night club sounds like a lot more fun than hanging out alone in a deserted park all night.

Question #4. After calming down from your night of feasting and carousing, you take a long walk to kill time before the sun rises. Up ahead is a castle with a gatepost with a crest and your name on it. Yes, you have found your vampiric castle. You are Duchess Veronique Van Cullen with vast new treasures. You enter the castle. What is the first thing that captures your attention?

A. The stairs leading to the basement, where you know you'll find the damp, the musk, the dark earth, and the coffins

B. The fine oil painting of the first Duchess Veronique Van Cullen, who "died" in 1232. You wonder where she is now.

C. The ankle-length, black-and-pink silk-and-lace gown that is custom made just for your body (and that of the first Duchess Veronique Van Cullen, whose measurements were 37–22–34). You are thrilled that your body is now so glamorous! With this gown, you are sure to attract any mortal male you want.

D. The black leather miniskirt with matching corset that makes you look even better than you do in the gown (see C, above). You try on the outfit. With the spiked black heels that you find beneath the oil painting, you look like a vamp sure to catch the guys.

E. An oil painting of the first Duke François Van Cullen, who is so handsome you almost faint. If you look like the first duchess, you know that there's a guy out there, just waiting for you, who looks like the first duke.

If you chose answer A, the stairs leading to the basement where you know you'll find the damp, the musk, the dark earth, and the coffins, you are a typical vampire. I don't expect you to have a very fun time for the rest of eternity. Why would you choose a damp, musky basement, and a coffin over any other option?

If you chose B, the fine oil painting of the first Duchess Veronique Van Cullen, who "died" in 1232, I'd say you're pretty smart. After all, she looks a lot like you, and in the vampire world, any girl who looks like a duchess from 1232 probably has a male vampire soul mate out there, waiting for her.

As for answer C, the ankle-length, black-and-pink silk-and-lace gown that is custom made just for your body, you're being too vain. Control yourself, girl! You have better things to do right now than tinker with some clothes. You already look like a duchess from long ago! You just inherited a castle! At a time like this, who cares about clothes?

You can probably guess what I have to say about answer D, the black leather miniskirt with matching corset that makes you look even better than you do in the gown. Save it for later, honey, and check out your new castle first.

Finally, answer E is a lot like answer B. Whereas in B, you

found that you are the incarnation of a duchess, in answer E, you find your duke. I'm hoping that you selected B first, then quickly looked from that oil painting to the one of the duke in E. Now you know that your soul mate, a gorgeous vampire guy, is waiting for you. You just have to find him.

Question #5. What are you most afraid of now that you're a vampire?

   A. Werewolves

   B. The sun

   C. Living forever all alone without the Duke François Van Cullen

   D. Sleeping in coffins

   E. Having to hunt for prey

This is a difficult question to answer, isn't it? I would rule out both A, werewolves, and B, the sun, right away. As a vampire, you can control wolves, and you really need not fear the threat of a werewolf pack. As for the sun, who cares? You can play all night, and besides, if you're anything like the Cullen family, some weak sunshine won't hurt you anyway. Answer D, sleeping in coffins, is no big deal, either, because most vampires sleep in coffins. Just make sure you have a soft pillow and maybe some nice music playing in the background. Answer E, hunting for prey, comes with the vampiric territory, so you'd better get used to it. Probably the worst fear for me would be living forever all alone without my vampire love (answer C).

Question #6. You wander through your castle, kicking rats aside and swiping cobwebs off your face. You come to a Victorian bedroom with a big, four-post bed and an adjoined study. Someone has recently slept in the bed, you notice. Curious, you enter the study, where you see two thrones, and in one of the thrones is Duke François Van Cullen! What does he look like?

A. He looks like Edward Cullen.

B. He is six foot ten inches tall, has gladiator muscles, a huge smile with pearly white teeth, glowing blue eyes, and black hair.

C. He is five foot two inches tall, has a concave chest and no muscles, a thin smile with pointed teeth, beady black eyes, and gray hair.

D. He is five foot ten inches tall, weighs 340 pounds, and as you enter the room, he's stuffing four entire chickens into his mouth.

If you answered anything except A, he looks like Edward Cullen, there is something wrong with you! Enough said.

Question #7. What do you say to your true love as you see him for the first time?

A. Come on over here, sailor boy! Mama's got a treat for you.

B. You can't talk. You just stand there, blushing and shivering.

C. Hey, nice seeing you, Duke ol' boy, are you a vampire, too?

D. Are you for real?

For those of you whose mothers never taught you the basics, never say this to a boy: "Come on over here, sailor boy! Mama's got a treat for you." This will make you sound as if you have been living in a dung heap in the middle of nowhere for your entire life. Never refer to yourself as "Mama" and never refer to a guy as "sailor boy." If you don't understand why I'm giving you this advice, ask your girlfriends or just take my word for it.

Some of you might answer that you'd stand there, blushing and not knowing what to say, which is answer B. I might do that. Or I might do answer D, which is to ask the duke if he's for real. I definitely wouldn't say A (see above) or C, "Hey, nice seeing you, Duke ol' boy, are you a vampire, too?"

Question #8. He says that he has waited for you and only you for well over seven hundred years. He has never fallen in love. Not since his beloved duchess died from consumption. How do you respond?

    A. Come on over here, sailor boy! Mama's got a treat for you.

    B. You can't talk. You just stand there, blushing and shivering.

    C. You tell him that you suspect that the two of you have a lot in common, both being vampires, and that you'd like to hang out with him—as much as possible. Then you swoon and faint.

    D. You have got to be kidding. What kind of fool do you take me for?

On Question #8, I have to go with answer C, or something very similar. I'll add that hopefully, you won't swoon and faint.

Question #9. There's a mirror across the throne room. You know better than to go near it. Do you think that you're going to miss seeing yourself in the mirror?

    A. Yes. You are *that* vain.

    B. No. Besides, you'd rather look at the duke.

This one's simple—answer B (you'd rather look at the duke) is the obvious choice.

Question #10. Would you mind turning into a wolf, a bat, and mist from time to time?

    A. The wolf and bat: I wouldn't like that at all.

    B. Turning into mist would be kind of cool. I could roil down the school halls and creep people out when I'm in the city.

It might be fun to be a huge mist rolling into math class one day and filling up the room. I could handle the wolf form when I need to save someone or command the pack, and I think I could handle the bat form for fast transportation in a pinch.

C. I would mind all of it. I don't want to be a wolf, a bat, or mist.

D. I'm beginning to wonder if I can transform back from vampire into pure human again.

The last question is the toughest one of all. Personally, if I'm being totally honest with you, my choice is C, I would mind all of it, and I don't want to be a wolf, a bat, or mist. But let's face it, if you're now a vampire, you don't have a choice. There's no way to do D, transform back into a human, so sadly, the only option is to live with it all: becoming a wolf, a bat, and mist from time to time.

CHAPTER 6

GOOD VAMPIRES AND BAD VAMPIRES

✧

Most vampires are presumed guilty before proven innocent. Case in point: Nosferatu, who was never even close to being a nice guy, and Bela Lugosi's Dracula, who always had a thirst for evil.

Nosferatu, originally meaning "plague carrier," came to mean "undead" much later. The use of the term *undead* implies something evil or sent by the devil. In an 1888 book called *The Land Beyond the Forest: Facts, Figures, and Fancies from Transylvania* by Emily Gerard, *nosferatu* was literally the term for an evil vampire. In Bram Stoker's *Dracula*, Professor Abraham Van Helsing, who is the expert on vampires and how to stalk and kill them, comments that the nosferatu do not die, but get stronger, and as they gain power, they become increasingly evil.

The 1922 movie *Nosferatu*, which we've talked about a little in this book, established vampires as evil figures of doom. It is a thinly disguised version of Bram Stoker's novel *Dracula*, for which the German Prana-Film moviemakers had not been able to procure rights. *Nosferatu* is set in 1838, which in reality, was the year a plague broke out in Bremen, Germany, where they filmed the movie.

Rather than a handsome, cute guy like Edward Cullen or a suave lady's man like Bela Lugosi, *Nosferatu* stars a vampire who is incredibly ugly and evil. Nosferatu, aka Count Orlock, is monstrous: he has long claws for fingernails, horrific fangs, an ancient bald head, and the overall look of a rat.

When Nosferatu, aka Count Orlock, arrives in Germany, he literally spreads the plague. He is the source of the plague, with the rats under his command and following his orders. This is evil personified.

Gary Oldman's version of Dracula in Francis Ford Coppola's 1992 film *Bram Stoker's Dracula* isn't nearly as evil as Count Orlock. Oldman is a handsome man about town in London, having been born centuries earlier as the first Prince Vlad the Impaler. Seeking his wife, whom he lost during his impaling, warlike years, Vlad Dracula sees a young woman in London who looks just like his long-deceased lover. Of course, the young woman is Mina Murray (played by Winona Ryder) from the original story by Stoker.

The Oldman character of Dracula shapeshifts into werewolves, bats, and other forms to attack people. For example, when he attacks Lucy Westenra, he is in the shape of a huge, terrifying werewolf, and the attack appears to be much more than a mere bite on the neck.

Yet the Oldman Dracula is somewhat sympathetic. Sure, he hacked off the heads of thousands of people back at Castle Dracula in the old ages. Sure, he impaled thousands of people on poles in the fields. Sure, he kills people, viciously attacks them, and drains them of blood, but still, he's a man in love. In fact, he is filled with loving devotion and affection for Mina, who represents his deceased wife. It doesn't hurt that Oldman is handsome, whereas Count Orlock literally looks like a withered, old rat-bat, depending on whether he is sleeping in bat form or just wandering around Castle Orlock like a rat.

We'll get back to Prince Vlad the Impaler in a minute. You may already know that Vlad, aka Count Dracula, was a real person. If not, you're in for a real surprise when you learn who he was, what he did, and how he became forever linked to vampirism. If you already know that Vlad Dracula was real, start pondering whether Edward and his family are anything like Vlad, and we'll get to the truth of that question shortly.

For now, let's rewind and talk about evil vampires through the ages. There were very few along the way who were at all good, though in recent times, some, such as Edward Cullen, have cropped up.

The reverend Montague Summers is mentioned in the Twilight Saga as a source of information about vampires. Curious about Edward and his family, Bella Swan searches the Internet for information about vampires and finds a quote by Montague Summers.

Montague Summers was a real man who wrote books such as *The Vampire: His Kith and Kin* in 1928 and *The Vampire in Europe* in 1929. His full name was Alphonsus Joseph-Mary Augustus Montague Summers, and he lived from 1880 until 1948.

His books explore vampirism around the world and throughout the centuries. He mastered everything there was to know about vampires: worldwide beliefs and folk legends, myths, anthropology, literary uses of vampires, and even theatrical versions. Summers believed vampires to be pure evil.

Summers's scholarly approach to the vampire noted that every recorded culture has traces of vampire beliefs, and that these vampires were not just evil men, but evil women, as well. The women became known as *succubi*, female demons who have sex with male humans. That's pretty evil, folks.

The succubi, according to the ancient Greeks, not only had sex with human dudes, but they also sucked them dry of blood (of course) and (brace yourself) ate the corpses! *Evil!*

As far back as ancient Greece, these vampiric monsters were associated with snakes and had the ability to shapeshift into bird form after filling up on human blood. In ancient Assyria and Babylon, the vampires were said to be lost, wandering souls of the dead who preyed on and sucked the life from humans because they had sinned during their own lives. In short, the Assyrian and Babylonian vampires were also evil.

The examples of evil vampires go on and on. Merely drinking someone's blood in the western version of vampirism is nothing compared to what vampires do in other parts of the world. The Ch'ing Shuh in China brings corpses back to life, and even eats both the corpses and the living in a cannibalistic feast from hell. The Indian Baital vampire is a corpse brought back to life by a batlike demon.

As for the real "Vlad the Impaler" Dracula, he was as evil as men can be. His father, Vlad Dracul (as opposed to the son, "Vlad the Impaler" Dracula), was born in the late fourteenth century and died in 1447. The older Vlad ruled Wallachia, which is today Romania, south of the Carpathian Mountains. He was the bastard son of Prince Mircea, who had ruled Wallachia before him.

By 1430, the older Vlad was in Transylvania in Sighişoara near the border of Wallachia. It was here that his second son, "Vlad the Impaler" Dracula, was born, and no, his parents did not call him Vlad the Impaler at birth; he got that name much later.

The older Vlad became a member of the Order of the Dragon, which intended to fight Islam. As Prince of Wallachia, the older

Vlad had trouble securing the throne, and to do so, he had to marry a second wife: Euphraxia, sister of Moldavia's ruler.

In 1437, Vlad allied his people with the Turks, but half a dozen years later, the Turkish army was defeated in war, and the Hungarians chased them through Wallachia. In the process, they also took the throne from the older Vlad Dracul. With help from his Turkish friends, he regained his throne, and to honor his relationship with the Turks, he gave them his sons, Vlad and Radu, as hostages.

Vlad and Radu were essentially imprisoned by the Turks, and Vlad became infused with the need to seek violent revenge from anyone who got in his way. Vlad also learned to disrespect and have no regard for human life. He was surrounded by immoral people, including his own father, who had sold him out and put him in great danger. He was so violent and cunning that his own guards were terrified of him.

When Vlad's older brother, Mircea, was tortured with hot stakes thrust into his eyes and then burned alive by the Hungarians, the throne of Wallachia was up for grabs. This was when the older Vlad had trouble securing his throne, for John Hunyadi, the Hungarian governor, put Vladislav II, from another side of the family, in charge. The Hungarians murdered the older Vlad, as well.

When he was approximately twenty years old, the younger Vlad fled to Moldavia in northern Romania. Years later, he returned to Transylvania, and oddly enough, sided with John Hunyadi when Vladislav II adopted policies that were favorable toward the Turks. Hunyadi was not a friend of the Turkish people. And Hunyadi ended up giving the Wallachian throne back to Vlad Dracul.

It is clear in Bram Stoker's *Dracula* that it was the real Vlad

Dracula who largely formed the basis of the fictional character. In the novel, Van Helsing states as much, saying that the vampire must be the Dracula who fought the Turks long ago. And once again, Van Helsing ties evil to the real Vlad Dracula, indicating the real person and his family were basically in cahoots with Satan.

The local Romanian peasants started referring to Vlad Dracula as "Dracula" because they considered him a *dracul*, meaning dragon or devil. Dracula literally means "son of Dracul" or "son of the dragon or devil." In actuality, Dracul and Dracula are nicknames, along with many variations such as Draculia, Dracole, Draculya, among others.

It's interesting to note that Vlad Dracula's descendants were considered evil, as well. Their nicknames reflected the popular feeling among their people that they were cruel and in league with the devil. There's an old saying, that the sins of the father are visited upon the sons, that is, if your father is "Vlad the Impaler" Dracula, people for generations are going to think of your family as satanic. For example, Dracul's son was known as Mihnea the Bad and another descendant was called Little Impaler.

When Hunyadi died from the plague in 1456, Vlad Dracula immediately traveled with his men from Transylvania back to Wallachia. He killed Vladislav II, took a formal oath of allegiance to both the Hungarian king and the Turkish sultan. He was now in a position to get revenge on anyone who had ever hurt or killed someone in his family. He ruled with extreme violence for six years.

On Easter day in 1459, Vlad Dracula feasted all day and then arrested all the ruling families who could have helped his father and brother. He considered them all responsible for the family deaths, and he decided to scare the hell out of anyone who might ever try to hurt a member of his family again.

He impaled the older men of the ruling families outside his palace. He left the impaled bodies there to rot and smell as a constant reminder to everyone not to screw around with him. Then he marched the rest of the ruling families to a town called Poenari, where he forced them to build a new chateau for him. This chateau became known as Castle Dracula.

If we can attribute anything remotely positive to Vlad Dracula, it might be that he gave the land and positions of the ruling families to the men who served him. And we have to keep in mind that his grandfather, father, and brother had all been murdered. Still, torturing and impaling people is more than cruel: it is evil.

In fact, even his own people were terrified of him, for Vlad kept impaling people until he became known as Vlad the Impaler. He even attacked the Orthodox and Roman Catholic Churches, with particular hatred for the Roman Catholic monasteries, which he viewed as havens for foreigners. If one villager did something to offend Vlad, he was known to impale every person who lived in that village. He took revenge to the level of insanity.

If foreigners seemed to ignore his trade laws, he invaded their countries, and impaled everyone he encountered. The impalements have been described, in particular by Radu R. Florescu and Raymond T. McNally in their books *In Search of Dracula: The History of Dracula and Vampires* and *Dracula: Prince of Many Faces, His Life and Times.* According to *In Search of Dracula*, which was published by Houghton Mifflin Company in 1994, the real Vlad Dracula was "an authentic human being fully as horrifying as the vampire of fiction and films—a fifteenth-century prince who had been the subject of many horror stories even during his own lifetime."[1]

A remnant of Castle Dracula still exists in Transylvania on top of the mountain where it was originally built by Vlad's tortured slaves. Surrounding the castle remnants are sheer cliffs that drop a thousand feet. There is indeed a Borgo Pass where Bram Stoker described it in his book. Central to our later discussions about Jacob Black, the area by the real Castle Dracula was filled with howling wolf packs at night, and the skies held bats that the villagers feared as demonic.

According to Radu R. Florescu and Raymond T. McNally, Vlad Dracula was so cruel that German, Turkish, Slavonic, and Byzantine people all thought of him as being, most probably, insane. He tortured and impaled people—men, women (even pregnant women), children, and babies—from all backgrounds, whether they were Hungarians, Germans, or Romanians.

But according to his people, he tortured humans in more ways than impalement. He burned them, axed off their heads, boiled them alive, and cut off their arms and legs. And he did much worse, if you can imagine it—such horrific tortures that I don't want to chronicle them here. When inquiring about his own afterlife, Vlad was told by a monk that even Satan would probably reject him from entering hell because Vlad was such a demented tyrant. Vlad was so insane that, according to reports, he not only killed and impaled the monk, but the monk's donkey, as well.[2]

---

1. Radu R. Florescu and Raymond T. McNally, *In Search of Dracula* (New York: Houghton Mifflin Company, 1994), p. 3.
2. Ibid., pages 80–87.

Clearly, the original and true Dracula, Vlad the Impaler, was evil beyond human measurement. Edward Cullen, and in fact, his entire family, have nothing in common with Vlad Dracula. Even the most nasty vampires in the Twilight Saga, vampires such as James, who *tries* to kill Bella; the Italian Volturi vampire clan, who *wants* to kill her; and Victoria (played by Rachelle Lefevre in the Twilight movie), who *could* kill her, are all pussy-cats compared to the real Vlad Dracula.

The bad vampires in the Twilight Saga cause a lot of trouble for Bella, basically because they want to drink her blood. But they're not exactly *evil*. They're dangerous and nasty, they put humans at great risk all the time, but they don't enjoy mon-strosities such as impaling, boiling, and cutting up their live vic-tims. They're just into blood lust.

To be a good vampire, as opposed to a bad or evil one, means that you don't try to hurt humans, whether you suck their blood or not. Moral vampires, like Edward and the Cullen family, even though they're lusting after human blood like crazy, drink the blood of animals.

Maybe the moral vampire equivalent of hooking up at a bar is hanging out at a blood bank. Maybe moral vampires head to the Red Cross of their local hospital after work to suck down a few drinks and get the evening started right.

There were a few moral vampires before the Cullen family came along. Vampirella, who was created by writer Forrest J. Ackerman, was a female vampire from the planet Drakulon in outer space. She first appeared in 1969 in her own comic book. On Drakulon, people drank blood instead of water, and Vampirella sported fangs, yet she tended to regret any harm she caused to humans.

ANNE RICE'S MORAL VAMPIRE

Anne Rice is the author of one of the most famous vampire books series of all time. Some of her vampires are incredibly handsome and romantic: totally seductive. They share some similarities with Edward Cullen, such as not wanting to drink human blood but being highly drawn to it. Edward is, hence, not the first of his kind, though of course, as a fully rounded fictional character, he remains distinctly unique.

Anne Rice's vampire character Louis knows that he must drink blood to survive, yet he considers killing humans to be morally wrong. He does not want to be evil, any more than Edward Cullen wants to be evil.

For four years, Louis drinks the blood of animals, just like the Cullen family, so he can avoid draining humans. But, as with Edward, his lust for human blood is much stronger than his lust for animal blood. Edward comments that drinking animal blood is the same thing for vampires as a vegetarian diet is for humans. Louis also finds only small satisfaction from animal blood.

In Edward's case, he keeps refusing to transform Bella into a vampire. He keeps choosing not to do evil, which means he resists the urge to drink human blood and make other vampires. In Louis's case, it is much the same. Finally, after four years, the urge to have human blood is too much for him to resist, and he returns to what he considers vampiric evil ways, yet he refuses to make new vampires after he transforms the character Madeleine.

Another Anne Rice vampire, Lestat, also faces the moral dilemma of good versus evil: drinking animal blood versus human blood. When Lestat was a human, he was very moral and good, and after being turned into a vampire, he fights with his conscience over the evil desires that now consume him. Anne Rice is a master of pitting good versus evil with her vampires. Her Lestat ends up sucking the blood of serial killers to use his evil for good purposes. Of course, Lestat eventually kills innocent humans because he cannot control his blood lust, and he realizes that he is a vampire, an evil entity, and this is simply his fate.

Earlier, before succumbing to his fate, Lestat seeks the ancient vampire Marius, who may help Lestat cope with his moral dilemma. In the Twilight Saga, Stephenie Meyer has Edward and the other vampires in one big "good" coven, the Cullen family. Edward does not go on a quest to find an ancient "good" vampire. Instead, he lives in quiet overcast places such as Forks, Washington, with other "good" vampires.

Marius is indeed a moral vampire in the Anne Rice series of novels. Marius devotes his eternal life to creating beauty in the world, figuring this may help offset his natural desire to do evil. In the fifteenth century, Marius was a nobleman who made religious paintings.

Another moral vampire was Barnabas Collins of *Dark Shadows* television serial fame. This vampire program was on television from 1966 through 1971, and then resurfaced in 1991. Barnabas, played by Jonathan Frid, made his first appearance in 1967 on episode 210. Barnabas needed blood to live, and he killed for it, as necessary. But he was a romantic figure who became extremely popular with female viewers.

It's worth noting here that werewolf Quentin Collins (whose

name comes from Quint in Henry James's novel *The Turn of the Screw*) and his descendants were all doomed to be werewolves. In the case of *Dark Shadows*, the vampire Barnabas and the werewolf Quentin came to understand each other. Jacob Black, a Quileute Indian, is the werewolf counterpart to Edward Cullen in the Twilight Saga. But we'll talk about werewolves and their relationships to vampires in a later chapter. For now, we're discussing some of the good vampires who predated Edward Cullen.

There's also a vampire called St. Germain, created by the very talented writer Chelsea Quinn Yarbro. St. Germain is four thousand years old and a lady's man with human emotions. He feels romantic bliss when he sucks human blood, yet he only needs a tiny amount of blood to survive.

The 1990s gave us Nick Knight, the good policeman vampire. (I'm not kidding.) The television program *Forever Knight* was extremely popular among vampire fans. The eight-hundred-year-old Nick Knight, played by Rick Springfield, lives on bottled blood so he doesn't have to resort to sucking blood out of necks. He actually rejects a long-term romance with a female vampire to try and become more human again.

Now along comes Edward Cullen, the epitomy of good vampires.

VAMPIRE.MATCH.COM QUIZ

Okay, we all know that there are plenty of online dating Web sites, where you can look at guys and assess their cuteness. Sometimes, people even meet and fall in love using online dating Web sites. So what if there was a vampire.match.com, and you went there one day, hoping to find the vampire love of your life.

Assume further that Edward Cullen was listed there (obviously not of his own doing). Assess your vampire readiness. Just how far will you go to be with the man of your dreams? How suited are you to be the love of Edward Cullen's life? Circle your answers, then tally up your score.

1. Would you be able to drink blood, and only blood for the rest of eternity? **Yes or No.**
2. Would you be willing to rob blood banks and hang out at the Red Cross rather than suck blood out of your friends' necks? **Yes or No.**
3. Would you be willing to hunt deer and bears at night to get your bloody dinner? **Yes or No.**
4. Would you want to live forever? **Yes or No.**
5. Would you be willing to kill people to drink their blood and keep up your strength and nutrition? **Yes or No.**
6. Do you like the color black? I mean, do you like black *a lot?* **Yes or No.**
7. Would it bug you to watch your former human friends and family grow ancient and die while you remained seventeen forever? **Yes or No.**
8. Would you feel comfortable turning your loved ones, the human loved ones, into vampires? **Yes or No.**
9. Would you be comfortable lifting cars and vans, running almost at the speed of light, and jumping over houses? **Yes or No.**
10. Would you be able to hate werewolves, even if they were your best friends? **Yes or No.**

(continued)

11. Is one of your best friends, now, a werewolf? **Yes or No.**

SCORING: To even get a second glance out of Edward Cullen on vampire.match.com, you have to score at least six points. Give yourself one point for each yes you answered for the following questions: 1, 2, 3, 4, 7, 9, and 10.

If you answered yes to question 5, you should find another vampire man. Edward's not for you. Even if you look like a supermodel and have the sweetest personality around, Edward doesn't want a girl who sucks human necks.

If you answered yes to question 6, you're probably not going to score with Edward. Remember, he's not a Goth, he's not particularly into the color black, and he doesn't wear a black Dracula cape, either.

If you answered yes to question 8, give up all hope of scoring with Edward or any vampire dude remotely like him. Edward most definitely does not want to turn his lovers into vampires.

Now, if you missed one and scored only six points, don't sweat it. Edward's a nice guy, and he isn't going to dump you over a measly one point.

As for question 11, if you answered yes to that one, give up all hope now. Let's face it, if one of your best friends right now happens to be a werewolf, you are a nutcase. Edward is too terrific a guy to saddle himself with a nutcase. So move on and pick another vampire, maybe Nick Knight or Barnabas Collins.

CHAPTER 7

SEXY WEREWOLVES:

They're Furry, Strong, and Sensitive New Age Kinds of Guys, So What's Not to Like?

✦

Everyone I've talked to about Edward Cullen agrees that he's just about the cutest guy imaginable. When I talk to fans about Twilight, most of them say two things: first, that they love the series because Stephenie Meyer is such a terrific writer; and second, that they're crazy about Edward Cullen. But what about Jacob Black, the young werewolf in the Twilight series? He's Bella Swan's best friend, and she loves him, too, just in a different way from how she loves Edward.

In the first book, *Twilight*, the Native American Jacob is fifteen years old, and Bella thinks he's innocent and naïve, too young for her really, though cute in the way he pursues her. It often seems that the boys who want us aren't always the ones *we* want. Even the nicest boys may not be the ones that girls think of in terms of romance. Sometimes, guys who are good-looking, sweet, and kind just can't make it with the girls they pursue. Look at Mike Newton, the cute blond boy who chases Bella throughout the first book. He's a nice guy, and she likes him, but only as a friend.

Romance is strange in this way. It's an attraction that can't be analyzed rationally with any sense of honesty. You either fall for a guy, or you don't. This is why people always say that love is based on chemistry and sparks flying. After all, "love at first sight" happens a lot, and you don't know a person when you first see him.

There's a huge market for relationship advice, including tips for guys about what girls really find attractive about them. Of course, there are what I would call chauvinist pig attitudes that girls just want guys who are rich and/or powerful. This is an absurd stereotype, at least according to my own feelings and those of just about every girl and woman I've talked to about the subject. The stereotype may work for women who are gold diggers, I suppose, but not for the rest of us.

Some relationship "experts" claim that girls subconsciously pick guys who appeal to them as potentially good fathers. Perhaps this is true when a girl is getting old enough to want to settle down, but this is definitely not the reason a girl falls for a guy. No way.

Other experts, including scientists,[1] believe that women want macho hunks while we are menstruating, but the rest of the time, we're happy with more feminine kinds of guys. Again, I've seen no evidence of this trait in any girl or woman I have ever known, including myself. It seems more likely that we choose sexy guys (that is, macho hunks) for sexual purposes, but when it comes to close friendships or long-term lovers, we opt for guys who are both macho *and* sensitive.

The scientific "experts" further theorize that women are even unfaithful to their men so that they can secure the "best" male genes for their children. Further, say the "experts," while it's cool to remain with a more feminine guy over the years, we also want flings with extremely macho guys at the same time.

---

1. For example, see http://news.bbc.co.uk/1/hi/sci/tech/376321.stm.

If the above is true, then someone like Bella would have a long-term boyfriend who is more like Jacob than Edward. She would keep Edward as her sexual fling and Jacob as her eventual husband or partner in life. In the first book, Edward is a macho hunk (albeit a sensitive macho hunk, a very rare find), while Jacob is sensitive, sweet, and caring. But how many of us would marry the first book's Jacob instead of Edward? Very few, I suspect.

Of course, once we see Jacob as a werewolf, it becomes impossible to think of him as at all feminine. He remains sensitive, sweet, and caring to some extent, but he also becomes hostile and aggressive in his werewolf stage of life at age sixteen. By the time of the second and third books, *New Moon* and *Eclipse*, he's almost like the Incredible Hulk or a guy on steroids: he can be nice, but he can also fly into angry rages, even in human form.

At age sixteen, Jacob is six feet seven inches tall and extremely muscular. He qualifies as a hunk, but still, Bella prefers Edward, and so do most readers. It's not that we dislike Jacob—we like him as a character and know he would make a great friend.

When Edward leaves Bella for a long period in *New Moon*, she starts hanging out with Jacob all the time. Jacob tells Bella that he loves her, and he even kisses her against her will. Most readers probably see this coming, as it's pretty obvious that Jacob has a crush on Bella from the first time we encounter him in the pages of *Twilight*. We learn that werewolves are extremely violent, have hot tempers, and when angry, transform from human into their werewolf states. They become furry and über-strong, yet in Jacob's case, they can also retain their human kindness and sensitivity.

Werewolves such as Jacob are furry, strong, new age, sensitive kinds of guys. So what's not to like? Do you think werewolves are sexy? If not, is it because they look like huge beasts? If you're not attracted to werewolves for this reason, then why are you attracted to vampires, who after all, can take the shape of wolves and bats?

Maybe it's because, when the werewolf physically attacks a woman, (1) he is in wolf rather than human form, and (2) he does not hypnotize her with his eyes and voice, nor does he inject a werewolf venom into her to anesthetize her to what he is about to do. When a vampire attacks, he does hypnotize his prey, he does anesthetize her neck, and he appears to her in highly romantic visions, usually of a strong, handsome man with mesmerizing eyes. Werewolves are just . . . *wolves.*

Whereas the vampire tantalizes us romantically, the wolf attacks us, pins us to the ground in beast form, and then feasts upon us, usually to the point of death. It's a gruesome death, as bad as being attacked, pinned to the ground, and eaten by any enormous, crazed beast.

The word *werewolf* isn't as easy to define as Dracula, son of the dragon-devil. If the word *were* means man, then *werewolf* means "man-wolf." In French, a werewolf is called a *loup-garou,* and while a *loup* itself is a wolf, a *garou* refers to a werewolf; so a *loup-garou* means "wolf-werewolf," which is a bit of an overkill, if you'll pardon the expression.

It was in 1212 when the first documented use of the term *werewolf* appeared, and then, in the early 1300s in a poem called *The Romance of William of Palermo,* the word *were-wolf* was used repeatedly. The poem was translated from twelfth-century French. Many experts agree that *werewolf* is derived from the concatenation of the words *evil* plus *man* plus *wolf.*[2]

In the 1941 movie *The Wolf Man,* starring Lon Chaney, lycan-

---

2. Ian Woodward, *The Werewolf Delusion* (New York: Paddington Press Ltd., 1979), pp. 238–240.

thropy is described as a disease of the mind that makes men think they are wolves. The Wolf Man's father hopes that his son has lycanthropy, that it's all in his head. After all, it's hard for him to believe that his son has literally turned into a werewolf. The sign of the werewolf in this film is the pentagram, the five-pointed star of the devil.

When Larry Talbot, aka the Wolf Man, returns home to his Welsh countryside castle to be with his father, we see him as a sweet, kind, considerate man. By today's standards, his methods of picking up girls are naïve and somewhat goofy. But he's a moral man, an upright citizen, a young man about town. Not incredibly handsome, he's very tall and muscular.

You might recall that Jacob Black is similar to Larry Talbot in the Twilight series. Jacob is also portrayed as a sweet, kind, considerate guy, his methods of picking up girls are naïve and somewhat goofy, he has high morals, and is a decent citizen. As for being a man about town, that's hard to do at fifteen, but much easier for Larry Talbot, who looks as if he's well into his thirties in the film. In the Twilight series, Jacob is not incredibly handsome, but he is tall and muscular.

Throughout *The Wolf Man*, the werewolf is described as a gentleman with a pure heart who transforms into a wolf at night, but only when the wolfbane blooms. Both Larry Talbot and Jacob Black fit the bill, except that Jacob becomes a werewolf when he becomes a "man" at sixteen. In *The Wolf Man*, when attacked and bitten by a werewolf, an ordinary man changes at night into the very type of beast that bit him.

Wolfbane is real, a plant with blue flowers that the ancient Romans called the *lycoctonum*. Lycanthropy itself comes from ancient Greek mythology, in which Zeus became angry with Lycaon and turned him into a wolf. But other ancient writers, such as Virgil, wrote that lycanthropy was caused by medical problems, such as depression and ingestion of drugs in some form. Lycanthropy has also been considered a genetic condition, in which a man's hair grows to excessive lengths all over his body. In older times, when a man was covered in what looked like fur, people assumed he might be a werewolf, and they took action: a silver bullet might kill a werewolf, or beating him to death with a silver-handled stick.

Wolfbane sap itself is a deadly poison that kills (you guessed it) wolves. In medieval times, villagers would hunt wolves with arrows tipped in wolfbane, and if a werewolf was hounding the people, they figured that maybe some wolfbane poison would do the trick. It was thought that even a bit of wolfbane on a door would scare the werewolves away, howling back into the night and far away from the village.

Larry Talbot eventually convinces the girl of his dreams to go to a late-night gypsy carnival with him. In old-movie fashion, he wears a fancy suit, tie, and hat, while she wears a tailored, tight-fitting, prim dress with high heels. They walk through the muddy forest, which is swirling in heavy mist. (In fact, if you watch the movie, which I highly recommend, notice just how much mist there is in the film. Probably half the budget for *The Wolf Man* was spent on humidifiers and other mist-producing equipment.) In old-movie fashion, although Larry appears to be at least thirty and the girl at least twenty-five, they must be chaperoned by the girl's friend.

At the gypsy carnival, an old fortune-teller, played by the famous vampire Bela Lugosi, sees a pentagram on the hand of the girl's friend and warns her that she will be killed by a werewolf. Wolves howl, there's wolfbane everywhere, and then before you know it, the friend screams, Larry runs after her, and Larry watches as a wolf rips out the jugular vein from her neck and kills her. Not a particularly romantic way to die, certainly not as romantic as having a sexy vampire *man* nibble on your anesthetized neck because he's highly aroused by the mere thought of you. No, the werewolf is quite different. He just rips out the girl's neck while she shrieks in pain.

Larry and the wolf fight, and the wolf bites Larry in the chest, and hence, Larry Talbot turns into a werewolf himself.

So let's summarize what we know already about the sexiness of vampires versus werewolves. I'll tell you which traits appeal to me, and you tell me which traits appeal to you.

VAMPIRES vs. WEREWOLVES: SEX APPEAL				
Trait	Vampire like Edward?	Werewolf like Jacob?	Is this trait sexy to Lois, the author of this book?	Is this trait sexy to *you*, the reader of this book?
Tall	✓	✓	✓	
So handsome he's like a god	✓		✓	
Moderately good-looking but only in human form		✓		
Extremely muscular	✓	✓	✓	
Clean shaven	✓		✓	
Very furry face		✓		
Greek god nose and profile	✓		✓	

(continued)

VAMPIRES vs. WEREWOLVES: SEX APPEAL *(continued)*				
Trait	Vampire like Edward?	Werewolf like Jacob?	Is this trait sexy to Lois, the author of this book?	Is this trait sexy to *you*, the reader of this book?
Giant snoutlike wolf nose		✓		
Delicate hands	✓		✓	
Paws		✓		
Long fingernails	✓			
Claws		✓		
Mesmerizing golden eyes	✓		✓	
Beady, beasty eyes		✓		
Furry body		✓		
Runs on two legs	✓		✓	
Runs on four legs		✓		
Smooth, soothing voice like honey	✓		✓	
Snarls, howls, and growls		✓		
Nibbles on your neck	✓			
Rips your neck out		✓		
Sensitive and caring	✓	✓	✓	
Passionately in love	✓		✓	
Loves you romantically, but doesn't ring your chimes		✓		
Immortal	✓			

At this point, you know what we have in common regarding our taste in men. I don't have a clue what you put in your column, but I'm hoping you didn't indicate that you think a guy who runs on four legs while he's howling at the moon is cute.

CHAPTER 8

WHAT TO EXPECT WHEN YOU FALL IN LOVE WITH A WEREWOLF

✧

Clearly, if your man's a werewolf, don't expect him to be home at night. He's out on the town, honey, and up to no good. Just face the truth.

As nice as he is, a werewolf like Jacob Black isn't going to be any better. He'll be out prowling every single night, and when he comes home, expect to wash up a lot of blood. He'll track it through the doorways or windows, he'll smear it on your carpets and floors, it'll get all over the sofas and walls. Face it, you're going to spend the rest of your life washing away blood every morning as if you're living with a serial killer.

Well, if you fall in love with a werewolf, you *are* living with a serial killer.

If you decide that you just have to be with a werewolf, make sure your clothes are made out of plastic or vinyl, or everything you own will be ruined by the blood. At minimum, wear plastic smocks over your regular clothes. Oh, and you might want to put those clear plastic furniture covers on all of the sofas and chairs, too. Plastic drop cloths used by painters are a good idea. Buy at least a hundred of them, and put them everywhere.

I hope you like plastic. A lot.

Aside from the plastic, invest in a lot of soap, so your man can scrub his victim's flesh and blood off his body when he gets home at sunrise. You'll need a lot of additional soap, too, for use after the household blood scrubbing every morning. Don't bother with white or lemon-colored washcloths; they'll turn muddy pinkish red soon enough. Just buy a few dozen towels and wash cloths in muddy pinkish red, and get used to the color.

I suggest you throw out your television, so there's no way you can watch the nightly news with the gruesome daily reports of vicious werewolf killings in your neighborhood. Disconnect from the Internet for the same reason. And when you go outside—anywhere at all—it might be smart to start wearing long veils and dark sunglasses. You don't want anyone to know it's you. Once people start seeing what your home life is like— husband out all night, every night, nobody ever allowed inside your house until you scrub it for hours, husband sleeping all day due to exhausting night routine, and so forth—your neighbors and former friends will start shunning you to the point where you are completely ostracized. If you don't start wearing the veils and sunglasses, you could even get stoned, so be careful.

Make your man brush his teeth and gargle with Listerine when he gets home at five A.M. Don't let him make any excuses. Force him to wash out his mouth, or you'll be inhaling his rotting meaty breath all day. How you're going to kiss this guy is beyond my comprehension.

Remember, you've fallen in love with a man who is, when you get right down to it, a cannibal. Yes, he rips out the throats of women. Yes, he devours their meat. He is a werewolf. There is no way around this fact.

In the case of Bella Swan, had she not ended up with Edward Cullen, she might have ended up with Jacob Black. The Quileute tribe in the Twilight Saga is an ancient werewolf pack, and they have always hated vampires literally to the death. Although Edward's family poses no threat to humans or even to Quileutes, aka werewolves, the pack hates the Cullens anyway. It is a blood feud, stretching back to the beginning of time, and most likely, continuing forever, unless in the fourth book Stephenie Meyer brings the vampires and werewolves together—but while I wrote *this book* after the first three books were available, by now we have all read the fourth book and should know the answer.

So right up front, we know that, should a girl such as Bella end up with a guy such as Jacob, she's going to lose the friendship of Edward and his entire family, for they are all vampires. She'll have to side with her husband, Jacob the werewolf, and his family.

Also, should a girl end up with a werewolf husband, she'd better keep away from him as much as possible. It doesn't sound like much of a relationship, does it? Given that a werewolf like Jacob is going to explode—at any moment—into anger and violence, his lover or wife had better learn, as quickly as possible, to (a) keep her distance, and (b) run fast.

Of course, if you fall in love with a werewolf, just as with a vampire, you never have to worry about walking through the woods late at night, alone. You are perfectly safe. If your man is a werewolf, and a vampire, mugger, beast, or rapist attacks you, wolves will come from everywhere instantly and kill your attacker. Your entire life could consist of long walks alone in the forest late at night. It beats being stoned by your neighbors, doesn't it?

Let's say your werewolf looks like a big version of Taylor Daniel Lautner, who has been cast to play Jacob Black in the Twilight movie. Taylor is sixteen, has thick spikey black hair, but he isn't six feet seven inches tall and packed with huge muscles. But we'll say that he's gotten taller and has been pumping iron, and we can easily see him as Jacob Black.

With Jacob being six feet seven inches tall and ripping into werewolf form every night, any girl who ends up with him is going to have to spend a lot of time in the men's department of her local store. Not only are his clothing sizes unusual, but he rips his pants and shirts every single night when his body zaps from human to monstrously huge wolf form. You might consider buying large men's clothes in bulk. Maybe you should just import them in warehouse-sized shipments from wherever they are made.

Rather than seeking a Goth look, remember, you're not with a vampire dude, you're with a werewolf. They are most definitely not waxy and pale. The thin, washed-out look is not their thing. So throw away the white cream foundation, the blue face tints, the reddish black lipsticks, the bronze contact lenses. You need a whole new approach to your makeup regime.

You have two choices. If you really want to attract your werewolf lover, then it might make sense to sprout some more hair, maybe even patches that look like fur (ugh). If you're more like me and you'd rather that the werewolf guy get nowhere near you, then forget the body hair and fur, and go for the tough-chick camouflage look instead.

But we're assuming that you've fallen in love with this Jacob-like character, so this means you want to be attractive to him, right? In *Eclipse*, Bella realizes that she loves Jacob, as well as Edward. It's just that she loves Edward *more*. And Jacob tells Bella that he'll be there for her no matter what happens between her and Edward. So Bella does love the werewolf, and if you should encounter a Jacob in biology class but no Edward, you could end up falling in love, too, but have no Edward to love *more*.

If so, you have your work cut out for you. Once your werewolf man is tucked into bed, snoring for the rest of the day, and once you've finished scrubbing up his bloody mess, you have a few hours to doll yourself up before he gets up for the night and maybe wants to give you some loving (major ugh).

It could be that, in the beginning, he liked you as a human girl, with ordinary skin, hair, and teeth. But over time, he may want one of his own kind, a werewolf-woman, and unless you want him roaming at night for more than a bite to eat, you'd better start transforming yourself.

Unfortunately, there are no simple ways to coat your body in fur. To increase hair growth, you might be forced to have testosterone replacement therapy, or in your case, being a girl, testosterone addition therapy. To look more like a wolf may require that you use illegal drugs, which I definitely don't recommend. So let's set aside hormones and drugs as beauty treatments for the wife of a werewolf.

What else can you do?

Some scientists predict that within the next few years, we might have baldness treatments that rely on hair multiplication and cloning techniques. Labs expect to reproduce follicle stem cells, then inject them into the scalps of bald men. You could try this route, when it's available, but having injections all over your body doesn't sound like much fun. As with the illegal male hormones and drugs, the injections aren't an appealing beauty routine.

Finally, you could try hair transplants all over your body, including your face. With this technique, a doctor would have to surgically remove strips of hairy skin from a male donor's head. Don't ask me why any doctor would do this for you. My answer will be: he is a lunatic. And don't ask me why any man would agree to have his hairy skin removed from his head, just so you can try to look like a werewolf-woman. My answer will be: he's a greedy nutcase. Assuming you can find this doctor-donor nutcase duo, settle in for a long time on the surgical slab. The doctor will have to graft the donor's hairy skin into *your* skin (major major major ugh). I don't recommend it.

Give up, and buy a werewolf costume. Put it on right before your Jacob wakes up, say at eight P.M. Hopefully, it'll work.

If you find that the costume isn't convincing enough to satisfy your werewolf's lust for one of his own kind, you could try eating meat that's as raw as you can stand it, say at eight P.M. Then when your man gets up for the night, you'll reek of bloody meat, which is his preferred scent.

So what do you do if you fall in love with a werewolf? I suggest years of intense psychotherapy!

CHAPTER 9

WEREWOLF QUIZ!

✧

Not many people want to be werewolves, but apparently, some (such as Jacob Black and Larry Talbot) have no choice. What would you do if you suddenly learned that you, like Jacob Black and Larry Talbot, are a werewolf? Let's find out how well suited you are to the werewolf life.

Question #1. Would you like to be bitten by a werewolf?

___ Yes

___ No

Question #2. Do you hurt people when they interrupt your feedings, I mean, your meals?

___ Yes

___ No

Question #3. Do you fly into rages? Come on, be honest. This is between you and . . . well, between you and only yourself, because I can't see your answers.

___ Yes

___ No

Question #4. Do you like wolves? Do you think they're cute and lovable?

___ Yes

___ No

Question #5. Did you see the movie *Dancing with Wolves*? If not, would you like to see it?

___ Yes

___ No

Question #6. If you saw *Dancing with Wolves*, how many times did you see it?

___ At least a hundred times.

___ I haven't seen it yet, but I know that this is a movie I want to watch at least a hundred times.

Question #7. Are any of your friends werewolves?

___ Yes

___ No

Question #8. When you wake up, do you smell strongly of feces, blood, and dog?

___ Yes

___ No

(Please tell me that you didn't answer yes to this question.)

Question #9. Does the full moon make you shiver with delight and anticipation?

___ Yes

___ No

Question #10. Do you tend to wake up every morning, totally naked and not knowing why?

___ Yes

___ No

Question #11. Do you howl? Often?

___ Yes

___ No

Question #12. What is your least favorite color?

___ Silver, as in silver bullets.

___ Any other color.

Question #13. Is your body especially hairy?

___ Yes

___ No

Question #14. Would you say that your body is so hairy that it's like having fur on your skin?

___ Yes

___ No

(If you answered yes to this question, please promise never to send your photo to me.)

Question #15. What's your favorite thing to do for fun?

___ Run through the forest, drooling, panting, and sniffing the air.

___ Crocheting doilies.

Question #16. In your opinion, what are people?

___ Beings with souls that must be protected at all costs.

___ Chow.

Question #17. When you get together with the pack, I mean, your friends, what do you do?

___ Fight each other to see who is the strongest.

___ Discuss calculus and Einstein's equations.

Question #18. Where are your family members?

___ In forests, though some are in zoos.

___ In apartments and houses.

Question #19. What would you do if your grandparents were really sick and about ready to die?

___ Let them go out in violent glory.

___ Put them in a nursing home.

Question #20. You see your mortal enemy on the bus. What do you do?

___ Attack immediately.

___ Offer to play a game of chess with him.

Unlike the vampire quiz, something tells me that you don't need an answer key to the werewolf quiz. If you answered those twenty questions truthfully, then you already know if you're fit to be a werewolf or not.

CHAPTER 10

GOOD WEREWOLVES AND BAD WEREWOLVES

✧

They're all good as humans, they're all bad as werewolves. It's as simple as that. Werewolves may not want to maim and kill innocent women, but they do.

But this is true for vampires as well, so it's not fair that we dismiss the poor werewolf as always bad when not in human shape. Let's take Jacob Black and his family as examples. Bella Swan's father, Charlie, is best friends with Jacob's father, Billy Black. With Edward gone, Bella finds solace in Jacob's friendship and goes so far as to think of him as her personal sunshine. They work on motorcycles, which of course, Bella hides from her father, who for a long time, prefers Jacob to Edward. It's often the case that fathers prefer young men like Jacob to hot guys like Edward for their daughters. Without knowing one is a vampire and one is a werewolf, most fathers might prefer what they perceive as a shy, nice, young guy to a handsome, adventurous guy. Most mothers might think more like their daughters about these choices.

It's impossible to think of Jacob Black as a bad werewolf, even when he's in wolf form. I honestly think of him as a Lon Chaney in *The Wolf Man* type of guy, as mentioned in Chapter 7. Even when Lon Chaney is in wolf form, he's tormented by the fact that he's a werewolf. He doesn't want to bite or kill people, but a strong animal urge inside of him forces him to act as the wolf. His human reason and morality are overcome by base animal instincts.

I'm sure you've heard the famous statement, "I think, therefore I am." This is attributed to philosopher René Descartes, who suggested that the mind and body are separated in many ways. Because you are a thinking creature, this implies that you exist as an individual entity, a physical being different from others. It is the root of what philosophers call selfhood.

Werewolves have this selfhood. They think, they are moral, they intimately know good from evil, and they intimately know their physical selves.

Lon Chaney's portrayal in *The Wolf Man* epitomizes these ideas. He fuses culture (his human form) to nature (his beastly form). He shows us clearly that selfhood is divided, that each individual battles inside himself with good versus evil. It's a very common theme in literature and films.

Clearly, like *The Wolf Man*, Jacob battles inside himself with good versus evil. He is a fusion of the primitive and the civilized, the instinctive and the rational.

But what about Jacob's family? Are they good werewolves, or bad werewolves?

VERY BAD WEREWOLVES

In 1923 in Germany, there was a terrorist group known as Organization Werewolf. While the terrorists spread and grew in numbers, they didn't do any enormous damage until the

(continued)

Nazis came into power. Most of them were arrested prior to Adolf Hitler's rise, and at that point, the worst of them joined ranks with the Nazis.

Towards the end of World War II, Josef Goebbels revived Organization Werewolf. The Werewolves' task was to terrorize and murder anyone who wasn't a Nazi. Even females in Organization Werewolf got into the action, dumping burning water on Allied soldiers.

At the Nuremberg trials, Nazi leaders admitted that the Werewolves were still operating under the leadership of Martin Bormann, private secretary to Adolf Hitler and head of the party chancellery.

As late as 1994, the Werewolves planned to bomb Russian theaters showing Steven Spielberg's 1993 movie *Schindler's List*, which dramatized the story of a real German man who saved a thousand Jewish people during World War II. These Werewolves, about 100 strong, claimed to be spawned from the original Organization Werewolf in Germany.

New Werewolves or old Organization Werewolves, all were bad, very bad werewolves, much worse than Wolf Man or Jacob Black.

Sam Uley leads the pack of werewolves. When in high school, Sam had a girlfriend named Leah Clearwater, but after Sam started turning into a human-werewolf, the wolf clan told Sam that he could never tell anyone he was a werewolf. At that time, Leah was human rather than werewolf.

Needless to say, this is not the kind of secret you want to hide from your girlfriend. Isn't it bad enough when a guy has a secret such as "my dad's an alcoholic" or "my brother dated your cousin" or, worse, "I cheated on you with your best friend"? But if a guy's secret is that he's a werewolf, considering that he has the potential to maim and kill you at any time, his secret is about as bad as they get.

Now, Sam dumps his girlfriend Leah and leaves her for a townie named Emily Young, who sports some nasty facial scars due to her boyfriend's hostile werewolf ways. Whenever Sam sees Emily's scars, he still feels terrible about what he did. She had been gorgeous before he attacked her in his werewolf form.

So Sam Uley doesn't seem to be a bad werewolf, either; certainly no worse than the Cullen vampires. He doesn't want to hurt anyone, certainly not Emily Young, but he can't help himself any more than Edward can control his urge for blood.

On the other hand, these guys sound like human abusive men, don't they? They maim, attack, and otherwise hurt their women, yet later, they're sorry about it, and their girlfriends stay with them anyway. As humans, they're not abusive; perhaps that's the difference. Still, as a human myself, I would not want to be abused by a werewolf and then have to forgive him after he destroys my face.

Perhaps the werewolf, Quil Ateara, isn't such a great guy. He's one of the few werewolves in literature who actually is happy that he gets to turn into a werewolf at night. He "imprints" with a two-year-old, which is not at all cool, and although he claims that he'll always protect her and be with her, it still doesn't make him a great guy (but that's just my opinion). When a werewolf imprints with someone, he falls in love forever and must stay with that person, who is basically his soul mate (love, marriage, children). If Jacob imprints with Bella, then she's his forever. If

Sam imprints with Emily, she's his forever. If Quil imprints with a two-year-old, well, she's his forever.

After reading the first three books in the series, we wouldn't know if, in Stephenie Meyer's world, a werewolf can imprint with a vampire.

Paul is possibly one of the most hostile members of the wolf pack. For example, when Jacob tells Bella about the pack, Paul explodes into werewolf form and tries to attack Bella. This doesn't make him into a bad werewolf. It means that he's the standard kind of werewolf, certainly not good but not "evil."

As for female werewolves, there's Sam Uley's former girl-friend, Leah Clearwater, who became a werewolf during the novel *New Moon*. Traditionally, most werewolves in literature and film have been male. The bloodthirsty, carnal, beast behavior of werewolves makes us think of them, somehow innately, as male. But these wolves have to mate, don't they? So it makes sense that there are female as well as male werewolves. In the Twilight Saga, becoming a werewolf means being born into the pack and then undergoing a late-puberty transformation. In Twilight, the trait of being a werewolf is genetic. As noted earlier, in most werewolf literature and movies, a man turns into a were-wolf if he is bitten by another werewolf. There is nothing genetic about the traditional transformation of man into werewolf. We assume that Jacob, Leah, and the others were babies and children before their transformations. This differs from the vampires, who are bitten to transform—they aren't *born* into the vampire clan, waiting around until their mid-teens to transform.

JAPANESE FOX MAIDENS

Fox maiden is a nice way of saying female werefox—a girl who turns into a fox. An old Japanese folktale tells of a man named Sang, who encountered a fox maiden when he opened his front door one night. He allowed the beautiful young girl to come into his house, already enraptured by her intense beauty. She called herself Lien-shiang, and although she was from the "red light district," an area of town known for licentious behavior, Sang fell in love with her.

She came to him every few nights and stayed until dawn. But one night, when he wasn't expecting Lien-shiang, he saw another beautiful young girl in his study at home. Sang was afraid of her, thinking she might be a fox maiden, one of a dangerous group of young werewolf girls that roamed his homeland. But the girl convinced him that she was quite harmless and in fact came from a very good family.

Now, Sang was naïve, to put it mildly. For one thing, if you were studying math for a test the next day, and you happened to look up from your desk at home (or the sofa, the kitchen table, or the dog's bed, or wherever it is you study), and you saw a gorgeous girl standing a foot away from you, wouldn't you wonder if (a) you were going crazy, and (b) she had broken into the house and was about to rob or kill you? But Sang didn't think any of those things. He did think, to his credit, that she might be a female werewolf (not the first thing that you or I would probably think), but he quickly dismissed the notion.

The girl claimed she'd been watching Sang from afar, pining for him, wanting him for a long time, and not being able

(continued)

to control her urges any longer, she had to have him that very night. In fact, she had to lose her virginity to him that very night. That this statement of hers didn't send off all sorts of warning signals in the naïve (and well, stupid) Sang is shocking. But he just figured he was a really lucky guy, and he settled down for an evening of debauchery and fun with this stranger who had materialized before him as he studied.

The following morning, the girl asked if Sang had other lovers, and he told her about Lien-shiang. The girl said that she and Lien-shiang must never encounter each other, for they came from different "classes." Leaving a magical shoe with him (another tip-off to the naïve Sang that something was seriously wrong with this girl), she departed with the warning that Lien-shiang must *never* see the shoe.

What would you do if a guy showed up, gave you his gym shoe and said, "Never show this gym shoe to your boyfriend. Never. Or doom will befall you both"? Personally, I would refuse the shoe and never see the weirdo again.

But of course, Sang didn't have much in common with me. After some evasion with both young girls, Sang was with Lien-shiang one night when the other girl hid near his house to see what her rival looked like. The "shoe" girl heard Lien-shiang tell Sang that he looked as if he'd been making love to a ghost, that he was, in other words, looking very ill.

The "shoe" girl entered the room and told Sang that Lien-shiang was a fox maiden. Lien-shiang admitted it and added that no harm would come to Sang by making love to a fox maiden. In true female cat-fight form, Lien-shiang retaliated by telling Sang that the other girl was a ghost who was sucking the strength from him, so much so, in fact, that he could die from it.

I'm sure you agree that Sang had terrible taste in women. And, as for the rest of us girls, isn't it bad enough that we have to compete with other human girls? Do we have to compete with werefoxes and female ghosts, too? Is there no limit to our competition?

Not that this Sang character comes across as particularly appealing. Studies alone all the time, never goes out, has no friends, has no hobbies, has two lovers at the same time, with one being a werefox and the other being a ghost. Quite a catch, huh?

Anyway, Sang became very ill, and the two supernatural girls both nursed him back to health. Although the ghost was in love with him, she said that she would leave forever in order to save his life. Lien-shiang, the werefox, was pretty happy about this and set up house with Sang, the fool.

Meanwhile, the ghost took over the body of a young girl who died (and of course, the young girl was beautiful, so moronic Sang instantly fell in love with her upon first sight). The ghost returned to Sang, but this time, she was not a ghost but rather, her ghost spirit was in a real human body. Sang fell in love with the reanimated corpse. (Well, we've established he's no genius, so this shouldn't come as a surprise to you.) Sang even married the reanimated corpse-ghost.

Meanwhile, Lien-shiang was still hanging around the house, playing the role of second-string lover to Sang. She bore his child, dying in human form in childbirth and returning exclusively to fox form.

So the fox was roaming around the woods for ten years, with the reanimated corpse-ghost married to Sang, and things seemed as normal as they could be for someone as

(continued)

weird as Sang. But then one day, the fox's spirit entered the living body of yet another beautiful young woman and returned to Sang's house.

The three of them lived happily ever after.

Can you imagine how Sang might have explained any of this to his ten-year-old son? "Yes, son, your mother died in childbirth, and I ended up with Brunhilda here, who no, don't be silly, was never a ghost. Yes, I know she's ugly, having a face rotted to the skull and basically no bodily functions, but I swear to you, son, that she's *not* a reanimated corpse. And while your mother did die in childbirth, as I've been telling you for ten years, she's back now, too. But she's not a reanimated corpse like my current wife. No no, my son, your mother was a werefox, who turned into a fox due to the shock of delivering you, but now she's stolen the body of a young girl and returned to us! You should be so happy!"

In today's world, this guy would be committed to an insane asylum, don't you think?

CHAPTER 11

VAMPIRES AND WEREWOLVES:

Can They *Ever* Be Friends?

✧

In the Twilight Saga, werewolves and vampires definitely do not get along. In fact, the Quileute tribe werewolves have hated vampires for as long as there have been Quileutes and vampires. Even with the Cullen vampires, who don't drink human blood, the werewolves don't budge: they hate vampires, and it's as simple as that.

The relationship between vampires and werewolves is found in folklore around the world and also in many movies and books. Long ago, it was thought that the only way to destroy a werewolf was with a stake through the heart followed by decapitation and burning: same as traditional folklore about destroying a vampire. Due to widespread fear of vampirism and werewolves, many supposed vampires and werewolves were killed. Lquis XV in France actually commissioned a report about vampire-werewolf exorcisms.[1]

Throughout Eastern Europe, people believed that werewolves were wolves inhabited by a man's soul. After a rampage of killing and eating bloody meat, the werewolf would be sated, and the man's soul would return to his body. You can see the correlation

---

1. Ian Woodward, *The Werewolf Delusion* (New York: Paddington Press, 1979), p. 149.

between the vampire and werewolf: both transform into other creatures (bat, wolf), both are men whose souls depart from their human bodies, both kill people, both drink blood, and both can transform from animal form (bat, wolf) back to human form. These parallels were the reason that people in Eastern Europe, particularly Serbia, thought of vampires and werewolves as the same horrific entity.

According to the folklore, unexorcised werewolves eventually turned into vampires. I'm tempted to tell a bad joke about werewolves who need more exorcise at the gym, but I'll spare you. Any joke I can possibly tell you about unexorcised werewolves is so bad that you would probably spit on this book and throw it on the floor, then stamp on it with both feet in hopes of exorcising the bad jokes.

Russians believed that wizards and werewolves who died turned into vampires. And in Greece, people believed that vampires who were werewolves before they "died" snatched babies from their cribs and drank the blood of dying soldiers in battlefields.

It's also interesting to note that vampires in most films and literature can transform into wolves. So werewolves can turn into vampires, and vampires can turn into wolves. Clearly, the two are extremely interconnected.

If they are this connected, maybe sometimes they can't tell themselves apart; that is, what if a vampire thinks he's a werewolf, or vice versa? At minimum, the vampire might find a female werewolf attractive, or a male werewolf might find a female vampire attractive. You'd think that vampires and werewolves would be great buddies rather than mortal enemies, as they are in Twilight.

Werewolves probably avoid attacking vampires for a few reasons. For one thing, the vampire body probably doesn't have a lot of blood in it, so the werewolf would remain famished after attacking and sucking the blood of a vampire. For another, if the werewolf dared to approach Count Dracula or Nosferatu and started trying to chew on his leg, I suspect the vampire would become instantly enraged and kill the werewolf by throwing the beast against a wall or halfway across a forest. Somehow, it's hard to imagine Edward Cullen allowing a werewolf, say Jacob Black, to nuzzle his leg and maybe nibble a few bites out of his thigh.

And, if we reverse the situation, it's hard to imagine Edward Cullen attacking the werewolf Jacob Black and sucking Jacob's blood. It's hard to imagine any vampire sucking the blood from a werewolf's neck. It's certainly not as sexy and romantic as thinking about the vampire sipping on the neck of a beautiful young girl.

The belief in werewolf-vampires is fairly widespread in some parts of the world. For example, in Haiti, people think of werewolf-vampires as one entity, the *Jé-rouge* creature (meaning "red-eyed creature"). Folklore indicates that these Jé-rouge werewolf-vampires attack women constantly in the need to transform as many people as possible to werewolf-vampirism. Further, once someone is bitten, she can never be part of ordinary human life again. Instead, she is tied to the werewolf-vampire pack forever and unable to continue her close relationships with humans.

It's possible that werewolves hate vampires because the vampires are sexier and more appealing to young, beautiful girls. It could just be a case of jealousy. If you think of a werewolf as the school bully and the vampire as the boy every girl wants in high school, then it's easy to see why the werewolf has it in for the vampire.

In the case of Edward Cullen and Jacob Black, one is a godlike boy with golden eyes, a heavenly voice, a sweet attitude, and an intense masculinity, while the other explodes into a massive brown wolf five times the size of a human with a muzzle and black eyes filled with hatred and violence. With both boys in love with the same girl, Bella Swan, it makes sense that the wolf Jacob might figure himself at a disadvantage when compared to the vampire Edward.

It's also possible that werewolves hate vampires because the vampires dominate and rule the wolves. It's like any boss versus subservient slave-worker relationship. The boss gives the orders, and the subservient slave-worker has to do what the boss wants. In the case of a vampire, when he gives orders to the wolves, if they don't do as he commands, the vampire destroys them. After all, to a vampire, his wolf-slaves are just supernatural dogs. Naturally, this would impose a good deal of hatred and resentment on the part of any werewolf for his vampire master.

In the case of Edward Cullen and Jacob Black, Edward doesn't dominate and rule Jacob in any way. It's a hatred that stretches far back into time, with a treaty in place to keep the peace as long as the vampires don't bite any humans. It's a territorial thing based on animal instinct. Perhaps werewolves resent that the vampires are feeding in their hunting grounds. How many bears can both werewolves *and* vampires eat around Forks, Washington?

Also, keep in mind that the werewolves in Twilight protect humans such as Bella from bloodthirsty vampires, so perhaps the werewolves hate the vampires for this reason, as well. They may view the vampires as killers of humans, whereas they consider themselves killers of other animals. The Twilight werewolves differ from other werewolves in film and literature in that they don't confine themselves to attacking humans. And of course, they differ from other werewolves in that they hate vampires rather than being aligned with them.

THE FULL MOON

Why is it that spooky things always happen when the moon is full? Specifically, why do men transform into werewolves during the full moon?

According to Jacob Black, he doesn't need the full moon to transform into a werewolf. All he needs is to get mad. But our real folklore tells us that men are more prone to madness and transformation when the moon is full. The folklore, as Jacob says, may not be accurate.

It is thought that the light of the moon is some form of catalyst that turns a man into a wolf. This would not have much basis in science, of course, but as noted, it has a lot of basis in human folklore. For example, the ancient Greeks and Romans believed that the moon was included in the realm of the underworld and all forms of dark magic. Over time, people believed that werewolves, witches, and other supernatural beings derived their power from the light of the full moon. But the beings could change shape all month, just as the moon itself could change shape all month.

In ancient Egypt, it was thought that the moon was the mother of the entire universe. In Babylonia, the moon was even more important than the sun, which is unusual for ancient cultures, where the sun reigned supreme over all. People in other parts of the world, such as Asia, also thought that the moon was more powerful than the sun because, at night, light is needed far more than during the day. This is a bit illogical, because the sun is *what* provided the light during the day, and the moon is a much weaker source of light.

(continued)

For every question in life, there are people who come up with many opposing answers, some strange, some even stranger, and some totally illogical. For example, there are people who believe that *humans* become more violent during a full moon. In 1998, a study indicated that prisoners always became more violent on the days directly preceding and following a full moon. In fact, according to a news report, "The full moon does make people more violent, according to a scientific study of prisoners in the maximum-security wing at Armley jail, Leeds."[2] The prison officer, Claire Smith, was quoted as supplying the reason: "The best theory I have heard to explain why this happens," she explained, "is that we are made up of 60 to 70 percent of water and if the moon controls the tides, what is it doing to us? The effects of the lunar cycle is something I'm very interested in and everyone has a theory on the subject."[3]

However, scientists dispute this theory. Dr. Eric H. Chudler of the University of Washington points out that "popular legend has it that the full moon brings out the worst in people: more violence, more suicides, more accidents, more aggression. The influence of the moon and behavior has been called 'The Lunar Effect' or 'The Transylvania Effect.' "[4] He further writes that the word *lunacy* is actually derived from the word *moon* in Latin. But contrary to popular belief, statistics do not support the notion that the full moon makes people, or werewolves, more violent. While

2. David Bamber, "Tests in Jail Show Moods Affected by Lunar Cycle," *Telegraph* at http://www.telegraph.co.uk/htmlContent.jhtml?html=/archive/1998/11/29/nmoon29.html.
3. Ibid.
4. Dr. Eric H. Chudler, "Moonstruck! Does the Full Moon Influence Behavior?" at http://faculty.washington.edu/chudler/moon.html.

there were more assaults and crime during the full moon, there was no real relationship between the full moon and aggressive behavior by patients in mental institutions, by nursing home residents, by prison inmates, by murderers (that is, the homicide count did not increase during the full moon), by people depressed enough to call suicide hotlines and crisis centers, and so forth.

Of particular interest to us, Dr. Chudler supplies the Web site urls of three reports about animals biting humans and the phases of the moon. One report tells us that animals bite humans far more during a full moon than at other times.[5] The other two reports say the opposite, that the phase of the moon really does not affect the rate of animal bites at all.[6]

---

5. C. Bhattacharjee, P. Bradley, M. Smith, A. J. Scally, and B. J. Wilson, "Do Animals Bite More During a Full Moon? Retrospective observational analysis," *BMJ*, December 23–30, 2000, at http://www.ncbi.nlm.nih.gov/pubmed/11124173?dopt=Abstract.

6. S. Chapman and S. Morrell, "Barking Mad? Another Lunatic Hypothesis Bites the Dust," *BMJ*, December 23–30, 2000, at http://www.ncbi.nlm.nih.gov/pubmed/11124174?dopt=Abstract, and C. E. Frangakis and E. Petridou, "Modelling Risk Factors for Injuries from Dog Bites in Greece: a case-only design and analysis," *Accid Anal Prev*, May 2003.

CHAPTER 12

FAVORITE TWILIGHT CHARACTERS AND VAMPIRES AND WEREWOLVES THROUGHOUT TIME

✧

This is your unauthorized companion guide to the Twilight Saga by Stephenie Meyer, so it seems appropriate to test your knowledge about the vampires and werewolves in the series. On the left is a list of vampires and werewolves. Some are from the Twilight Saga, some are from other popular books and movies. On the right is a list of simple traits and descriptions that match up with the names on the left. Write the number of each character (Edward Cullen is number 1, of course) next to the trait associated with him or her. So, for example, if you scan down the right-hand list and find "has molten golden eyes," you might want to write a "1" next to that trait.

After you finish, I'll give you all the answers, so you can determine how much you know about the Twilight characters. Good luck! (I write, good luck, because I'm going to try to make this very hard. I know you are all huge fans of Twilight, so this game could be very simple; that is, unless I go out of my way to make it über-difficult.)

Character	Trait or Mini-Description
1. Edward Cullen	___ Loves Bella Swan, hates Edward Cullen
2. Lucy Westenra	___ One of the first vampires in film, an extremely ancient and hideous-looking creature
3. Varney the Vampire	___ A female vampire, tries to kill Bella
4. "Vlad the Impaler" Dracula	___ Plays Alice in the Twilight movie
5. Isabella Marie Swan	___ Very vain, soul mate is Emmett Cullen
6. Fox Maiden	___ Plays Carlisle in the Twilight movie
7. Stephenie Meyer	___ A practicing doctor of medicine
8. Eric H. Chudler	___ Plays Rosalie in the Twilight movie
9. Jacob Black	___ Loves Bella Swan, hates Jacob Black
10. J. R. R. Tolkien	___ Lien-shiang in a Japanese werefox folktale
11. Old Shep, the Sheep Dog	___ Gets injured a lot, falls in love with a vampire and a werewolf
12. Abraham Van Helsing	___ The vampire in *Dark Shadows*
13. Montague Summers	___ First appeared in a comic book, a female vampire created by Forrest J. Ackerman
14. Alice Cullen	___ Edward Cullen in the Twilight movie
15. Jonathan Harker	___ Knows a lot about violence during the full moon
16. Robert Pattinson	___ An extremely muscular vampire
17. Kristen Stewart	___ A giant wolflike dog who lived behind Lois's house before being run over by a tractor

(continued)

Character	Trait or Mini-Description
18. Jasper Hale	___ Mid-1840s vampire novel starring Sir Francis Varney
19. Taylor Lautner	___ Plays Bella Swan in the Twilight movie
20. Rosalie Hale	___ Can see the future and looks like a pixie
21. Rachelle Lefevre	___ Wrote the extremely famous *Interview with the Vampire* in 1976
22. Emmett Cullen	___ The amazing author of the Twilight series!
23. Larry Talbot	___ Vampires of Italy
24. Dr. Carlisle Cullen	___ Wrote *The Vampire in Lore and Legend;* Bella Swan reads excerpts from his work on the Internet
25. Nikki Reed	___ Alice's soul mate, was in southern vampire wars
26. Bram Stoker	___ Plays Jacob Black in the Twilight movie
27. Esme Cullen	___ The most famous werewolf of all time, played by Lon Chaney
28. Ashley Greene	___ Attacked Bella, was killed by Jacob Black
29. Anne Rice	___ A very handsome vampire, as handsome as Edward Cullen, but first appeared in a book by Anne Rice in 1976
30. Charlie Swan	___ Wrote *The Hobbit*
31. Bill Ramsey	___ In Bram Stoker's *Dracula*, a very attractive and flirtatious young woman
32. Embry Call	___ The human who turned into the Wolf Man
33. Barnabas Collins	___ Called the Werewolf of London, he acted like a werewolf and was "exorcised" for the malady

Character	Trait or Mini-Description
34. Sam Uley	___ Medical doctor's wife
35. Mina Murray	___ The real Dracula from the 1400s
36. Vampirella	___ English solicitor who travels to Transylvania to meet Count Dracula
37. Seth Clearwater	___ Sam left her for Emily
38. Leah Clearwater	___ Named after Stephenie Meyer's brother
39. Vlad Dracul	___ Jonathan Harker's fiancée
40. Nosferatu	___ Wrote the most famous vampire novel of all time
41. Mike Newton	___ Police chief
42. Peter Facinelli	___ A Nazi group of werewolf-men
43. Lestat de Lioncourt	___ Vampire hunter in Bram Stoker's *Dracula*
44. Angela Weber	___ Vlad the Impaler's father
45. Wolf Man	___ Leader of werewolf pack
46. Victoria	___ Plays James in the Twilight movie
47. Cam Gigandet	___ Has a crush on Bella, but is pure human
48. Laurent	___ Plays Victoria in the Twilight movie
49. Organization Werewolf	___ Good friend of Bella's, but not her best friend
50. The Volturi	___ His mother is not a member of the werewolf Indian tribe

Now check your answers with the ones below. If you missed anything that has nothing to do with the Twilight Saga, don't sweat it. The important thing is to know your Twilight characters, the rest can come later.

THE ANSWERS

Character	Trait or Mini-Description
1. Edward Cullen	_9_ Loves Bella Swan, hates Edward Cullen
2. Lucy Westenra	_40_ One of the first vampires in film, an extremely ancient and hideous-looking creature
3. Varney the Vampire	_46_ A female vampire, tries to kill Bella
4. "Vlad the Impaler" Dracula	_28_ Plays Alice in the Twilight movie
5. Isabella Marie Swan	_20_ Very vain, soul mate is Emmett Cullen
6. Fox Maiden	_42_ Plays Carlisle in the Twilight movie
7. Stephenie Meyer	_24_ A practicing doctor of medicine
8. Eric H. Chudler	_25_ Plays Rosalie in the Twilight movie
9. Jacob Black	_1_ Loves Bella Swan, hates Jacob Black
10. J. R. R. Tolkien	_6_ Lien-shiang in a Japanese werefox folktale
11. Old Shep, the Sheep Dog	_5_ Gets injured a lot, falls in love with a vampire and a werewolf
12. Abraham Van Helsing	_33_ The vampire in *Dark Shadows*
13. Montague Summers	_36_ First appeared in a comic book, a female vampire created by Forrest J. Ackerman
14. Alice Cullen	_16_ Edward Cullen in the Twilight movie
15. Jonathan Harker	_8_ Knows a lot about violence during the full moon
16. Robert Pattinson	_22_ An extremely muscular vampire
17. Kristen Stewart	_11_ A giant wolflike dog who lived behind Lois's house before being run over by a tractor

Character	Trait or Mini-Description
18. Jasper Hale	_3_ Mid-1840s vampire novel starring Sir Francis Varney
19. Taylor Lautner	_17_ Plays Bella Swan in the Twilight movie
20. Rosalie Hale	_14_ Can see the future and looks like a pixie
21. Rachelle Lefevre	_29_ Wrote the extremely famous *Interview with the Vampire* in 1976
22. Emmett Cullen	_7_ The amazing author of the Twilight series!
23. Larry Talbot	_50_ Vampires of Italy
24. Dr. Carlisle Cullen	_13_ Wrote *The Vampire in Lore and Legend;* Bella Swan reads excerpts from his work on the Internet
25. Nikki Reed	_18_ Alice's soul mate, was in southern vampire wars
26. Bram Stoker	_19_ Plays Jacob Black in the Twilight movie
27. Esme Cullen	_45_ The most famous werewolf of all time, played by Lon Chaney
28. Ashley Greene	_48_ Attacked Bella, was killed by Jacob Black
29. Anne Rice	_43_ A very handsome vampire, as handsome as Edward Cullen, but first appeared in a book by Anne Rice in 1976
30. Charlie Swan	_10_ Wrote *The Hobbit*
31. Bill Ramsey	_2_ In Bram Stoker's *Dracula,* a very attractive and flirtatious young woman

(continued)

Character	Trait or Mini-Description
32. Embry Call	_23_ The human who turned into the Wolf Man
33. Barnabas Collins	_31_ Called the Werewolf of London, he acted like a werewolf and was "exorcised" for the malady.
34. Sam Uley	_27_ Medical doctor's wife
35. Mina Murray	_4_ The real Dracula from the 1400s
36. Vampirella	_15_ English solicitor who travels to Transylvania to meet Count Dracula
37. Seth Clearwater	_38_ Sam left her for Emily
38. Leah Clearwater	_37_ Named after Stephenie Meyer's brother
39. Vlad Dracul	_35_ Jonathan Harker's fiancée
40. Nosferatu	_26_ Wrote the most famous vampire novel of all time
41. Mike Newton	_30_ Police chief
42. Peter Facinelli	_49_ A Nazi group of werewolf-men
43. Lestat de Lioncourt	_12_ Vampire hunter in Bram Stoker's *Dracula*
44. Angela Weber	_39_ Vlad the Impaler's father
45. Wolf Man	_34_ Leader of werewolf pack
46. Victoria	_47_ Plays James in the Twilight movie
47. Cam Gigandet	_41_ Has a crush on Bella, but is pure human
48. Laurent	_21_ Plays Victoria in the Twilight movie
49. Organization Werewolf	_44_ Good friend of Bella's, but not her best friend
50. The Volturi	_32_ His mother is not a member of the werewolf Indian tribe

CHAPTER 13

PROTECTING YOUR VAMPIRE, PART 1:

Everything You Need to Know About Fangs,
Sunlight, Crosses, Garlic, and Holy Water

✧

In the first book, *Twilight*, Bella Swan searches the Internet for information about vampires. She discovers several things that she remembers from horror movies. Some match Jacob's descriptions of vampires, that they have cold skin, live forever, and drink blood; and most important to Jacob, that vampires and werewolves are fierce enemies. Some match the descriptions we're accustomed to seeing in popular books and films, such as that vampires cannot handle the sun and sleep in coffins during the day. Much later, Bella learns more about vampires from Edward.

This chapter will explore the myths about vampires, in general, and how they relate to the characters in the Twilight Saga. We'll find that Stephenie Meyer creates characters quite different from traditional vampires, and they do not share many of the traditional traits of vampires.

First, let's talk about fangs. These are a staple of almost all vampires. For example, in the original Bram Stoker's *Dracula*, one of Jonathan Harker's first impressions of Count Dracula was that the vampire had sharp white teeth that protruded over his lips. He later described Dracula as having long, sharp canine teeth: fangs. The female vampires in *Dracula* also had fangs, and of course, any vampire who bit a human left two big marks on the victim's neck.

I've always wondered why the two vampire bite marks are so close together on the victim's neck. In film, the marks always appear to be perhaps a quarter to a half inch apart. Run your tongue over your top teeth. How far apart are your "canines"? There are four teeth between the two longest, sharpest teeth in your top gum. *Four teeth.* So if you were to bite into a sandwich, or say a neck, the two bite marks would be much farther apart than a mere quarter to half inch.

Even before Bram Stoker, vampire authors gave their characters fangs. The author James Malcolm Rymer, who wrote *Varney the Vampire*, supplied his vampire with fanglike teeth that plunged into the victim's neck, leaving two tiny punctures very close together.

My old favorite creepy vampire, Nosferatu, had incredibly long fangs, but his were not the canines but rather protruded more from the center front of his mouth. This would make Nosferatu's puncture wounds more closely spaced than those of Dracula's and most other vampires.

Anne Rice's vampires all have fangs, though in the case of Louis, the fangs grew slowly after he was transformed into a vampire, so he had to rip his victims' necks to drink their blood.

Bela Lugosi's portrayal of Count Dracula in the 1931 classic movie had sterling teeth—but no evidence of actual fangs. Lugosi's Dracula did not wear fake fangs for the movie, and neither did Lon Chaney, who later played the role of the vampire in *Son of Dracula* in 1943. Of course, these vampires left puncture wounds on the necks of their victims, so they clearly had long, sharp pointed teeth, such as those of the vampires in the Twilight Saga.

It's not always necessary for a vampire to have actual fangs.

Edward's teeth are more like the ones of Bela Lugosi and Lon Chaney, the original vampire masters. In *Twilight*, Edward even makes fun of humans who think they're cool and vampirish because they're wearing fake fangs. He thinks it's all very silly. Edward's teeth are as sharp as razors and sterling white: but no fangs, folks.

It must be difficult for a vampire with razor-sharp teeth to kiss his human girlfriend. He has to make sure that he doesn't slice and dice her lips, for example. And imagine a kiss between two vampires, one male and the other female, both with razor-sharp teeth. It could result in two pretty messed-up faces. Luckily for Bella, Edward Cullen has remarkable restraint and control, plus he's a perfect gentleman, so she is never hurt when he kisses her.

In 1958, an actor named Christopher Lee portrayed a very long-fanged vampire in the movie *The Horror of Dracula*. Lee's vampire set the pace for many years to come, with vampires opening their mouths wide, as if at the dentist, and baring their fangs. Ever since then, vampire costumes for Halloween, vampire book covers, vampire puppets, and Goths who think of themselves as vampiric have had fangs. The fangs are a vampire convention.

As fans of the Twilight Saga, do you like the fact that Stephenie Meyer did not follow the vampire convention of supplying Edward with fangs? Would Edward have been sexier with fangs?

My take is that Stephenie Meyer's fangless Edward is perfect—without the fangs. As Edward himself suggests, the fangs are silly myths.

The fangs might make a vampire more horrific, such as in the movie *Nosferatu*, but when your vampire is supposed to be romantic, charming, and Mr. Perfect, you don't really want him to be horrific. You want him to be enticing at all times. Edward Cullen is not a scary vampire, he's the vampire any girl would want.

There are even retractable vampire fangs in many films. In this way, the vampire appears normal except when feeding. The fangs slide down from the upper gums, then slide back up after the blood is slurped. This is even more silly than having two-inch-long fangs sticking out of your mouth at all times.

If you end up falling in love with an ordinary vampire who has fangs, just keep a lot of dental floss and toothpaste in the house. Especially if he has retractable fangs that stay inside his gums most of the time. Bloody fangs could be prone to some pretty nasty cavities and rot. You may want to try to convince your vampire man to use an electric toothbrush and gargle with Listerine.

If your vampire man is more like Edward Cullen, without the fangs, you don't have quite as much to worry about. As normal humans grow older, their teeth start chipping and growing weak, but with an immortal, it's safe to assume that a vampire like Edward will have strong teeth forever. There's no need to file the teeth to keep them sharp, as you might do with a kitchen knife. All you have to do is protect your lips and mouth from the razor edges, and you'll be fine.

ARE YOU OBSESSED WITH EDWARD CULLEN?

I'm assuming that every reader of this book is obsessed with Edward Cullen, especially now that Robert Pattinson is playing the role in the movie. But let's find out *how* obsessed you are with Edward. Answer the following questions, then tally your score as described after the quiz.

Question #1. How many times have you read the first book, *Twilight*?

   A. Only once.

   B. About half a dozen times.

   C. So many times I can't remember.

Question #2. How many times have you read the second book, *New Moon*?

   A. Only once.

   B. About half a dozen times.

   C. So many times I can't remember.

Question #3. How many times have you read the third book, *Eclipse*?

   A. Only once.

   B. About half a dozen times.

   C. So many times I can't remember.

Question #4. The fourth book was available on August 2, 2008. When did you read the fourth book?

   A. On August 2, 2008.

   B. I haven't read it yet, but I intend to read it right away.

   C. I probably won't get around to reading the book for a long time, if ever.

Question #5. When you're on the Internet, how often do you search for information about Edward Cullen?

   A. Constantly.

   B. Sometimes, but usually, I search for information related

(continued)

to my homework or how to crochet doilies and take care of swallows.

C. Never.

Question #6. If you have a boyfriend, since reading *Twilight*, what has happened to your relationship?

A. I have pretended my boyfriend is Edward Cullen, but I'm afraid to admit it to him.

B. I had to dump my boyfriend because I love Edward Cullen more and that will never change.

C. Out of desperation to keep me, my boyfriend dyed his hair, started working out in the gym, and got golden contact lenses. It didn't work. I still love Edward Cullen more.

Question #7. What do you dream about at night?

A. Edward Cullen.

B. Being Bella Swan, so I can marry Edward Cullen.

C. Both of the above.

Question #8. If you could be any character from any book that you've ever read, who would you choose?

A. I would want to be Harry Potter.

B. I would want to be Serena from the Gossip Girl series.

C. I would want to be Bella Swan. Obviously.

Question #9. What is your name?

A. Bella Swan.

B. Oops, I mean it's whatever-your-name-really-is.

Question #10. What's the perfect age for the perfect boyfriend?

A. Seventeen going on anything over a hundred.

B. Seventeen.

It's pretty obvious how to score this quiz, but some of you may not be as mesmerized by Edward as you think. So let's tally up your points and discover the truth.

THE ANSWERS

Question #1. [How many times have you read the first book, *Twilight*?] If you chose C, so many times I can't remember, give yourself one point.

Question #2. [How many times have you read the second book, *New Moon*?] If you chose C, so many times I can't remember, give yourself one point.

Question #3. [How many times have you read the third book, *Eclipse*?] If you chose C, so many times I can't remember, give yourself one point.

Question #4. [The fourth book was available on August 2, 2008. When did you read the fourth book?] If you chose A, on August 2, 2008, give yourself one point. Sorry, even if you chose B, I haven't read it yet, but I intend to do so right away, you cannot score a point for this question.

Question #5. [When you're on the Internet, how often do you search for information about Edward Cullen?] Clearly, if you

(continued)

chose A, constantly, then you get one point. If you're searching the Internet for doily or swallow information instead of
the latest gossip about Edward Cullen, you're not as obsessed
with him as you should be!

Question #6. [If you have a boyfriend, since reading *Twilight*,
what has happened to your relationship?] If you chose any
answer, A, B, or C, give yourself one point.

Question #7. [What do you dream about at night?] The only
answer worth one point is C, both of the above. You dream
about Edward Cullen, and you dream about being Bella Swan,
so you can marry him someday.

Question #8. [If you could be any character from any book
that you've ever read, who would you choose?] Some girls
might choose B, Serena from the Gossip Girl series. She and
Blair, from the same series of books, are both very popular. If
you selected A, that you want to be Harry Potter, then I assume you like magic a lot, but you do not get a point for being obsessed with Edward Cullen. If you chose C, that you
would be Bella Swan, you get one point.

Question #9. [What is your name?] If you chose either A or B,
give yourself a point.

Question #10. [What's the perfect age for the perfect
boyfriend?] The clear answer is A, seventeen going on anything over a hundred is the perfect age for the perfect boyfriend. If you selected A, you get one point.

Now add up your points. If your total is 10, you are clearly in love with the Twilight Saga and with Edward Cullen. If your total is 8 or 9, you're obsessed with Edward but there's still hope for your boyfriend. If your total is 5, 6, or 7, you like Edward but you're not obsessed with him. Anything from 1 to 4 means that you need to read the entire Twilight series again at least six times.

We've covered fangs and the vampires in Twilight, and once again, we've probed your devotion to Edward. True Twilight fans know that you can never talk enough about Edward or be too devoted to him. He's worth thinking about constantly, no matter where you are and what you're doing.

One thing that struck me right away about Edward is that he goes outside during the day. Sunlight doesn't seem to burn him into nothingness, as it does to most vampires. In fact, he tells Bella at one point that it's simply a myth that vampires are burned by the sun.

Of course, if you live in a constantly overcast place like Forks, Washington, there's not enough sunlight to fry you. Trust me, nobody needs SPF 50 in Forks. Nobody gets sunburned there. So it's the perfect place for a vampire family to live. They can go outside all the time without encountering any real sunshine. But in broad daylight, at high noon, beware, for you could fry into nothingness. Remember what happens to Edward in Italy, when he travels there and then plots his own demise. The bright high noon sun makes his skin sparkle, attracting all kinds of notice, and for this crime, he assumes the Volturi vampire clan will kill him.

While we're accustomed to thinking of vampires as hating the sun, it hasn't always been the case in folklore. In the early *Varney the Vampire*, for example, Sir Francis Varney has no trouble walking around outside during the day. Varney's real name before turning into a vampire was Mortimer, and he lived in London in the mid-1600s when human. He accidentally killed his own son, then was hit by lightning and passed out. When he awakened, Varney was next to an open grave and heard a voice telling him that he would forever be a vampire because he had sinned so badly by killing his son. Varney is much like Edward in that he walks in sunlight, has enormous strength, and does not need to drink blood constantly to sustain himself.

In 1819, the writer John Polidori wrote a short story called "The Vampyre," which starred the vampire Lord Ruthven. In this story, derived from a fragment penned by Lord Byron, the vampire is a pale Londoner who is very popular with girls. Lord Ruthven travels freely around the world with his human friend Aubrey, and sunlight does not seem to bother Ruthven at all. At one point, Ruthven is killed by thieves, who leave him exposed to moonlight, which somehow heals him. Ruthven ends up seducing and killing Aubrey's sister, after which he disappears and the tale ends. Lord Ruthven is similar to Edward in that he also walks in sunlight, but Ruthven's tale has the added twist that moonlight brings him back to life.

Then there's Carmilla, another vampire who walks freely during the day without being burned to shreds by the sun. Written by Sheridan Le Fanu in 1872, "Carmilla" was a short story featuring the female vampire Carmilla, who feeds upon a young girl named Laura. Carmilla looks like a painting of Countess Mircalla Karnstein that hangs in the castle where Laura lives. While Carmilla is very pale, it takes a long time for anyone to realize that she is a vampire. Her fangs are more like two needles, but usually are not visible to people. While she prefers the night, Carmilla can function freely during the day, similar to Lord Ruthven, Varney, and Edward.

Like many other vampires, Carmilla possesses enormous superhuman strength and can transform into different shapes, such as a wolf and a bat, though in Carmilla's case, she prefers to turn into a cat. She does sleep in a coffin near her family castle, and she preys on people close to her, both very much unlike Edward.

However, as noted earlier, when it comes to sunlight, most vampires are not at all like Edward. In Bram Stoker's *Dracula*, the definitive fictional volume about vampires, Count Dracula cannot function well during the day. But he can function a bit, transforming himself at sunrise, sunset, or even at noon. He is weak during the day but does not sizzle into nothingness.

It was in *Nosferatu*, which attempted to tell the Dracula story on film without having the rights to Bram Stoker's *Dracula*, that the vampire became the nocturnal creature of today's popular culture. In *Nosferatu*, Count Orlock (the Dracula wannabe) is killed by the sun as dawn first rises in the morning. After lusting for the blood of Ellen Hutter (the Stoker–Mina Murray wannabe character), Nosferatu is finally allowed to drain her neck one night. He is so filled with desire that he remains fixed, all night, at her bedside, teeth clamped into her neck, draining the life from her body. She willingly sacrifices herself in this hideous manner to save the world from Count Orlock, for she knows that, at sunrise, he will perish.

In 1943, Bela Lugosi appeared in *The Return of the Vampire*, in which the vampire Armand Tesla is killed by sunlight. Rather than disappearing in a wisp of smoke like Nosferatu, Armand Tesla dies because the sun melts his face.

After that, sunlight was used as the instrument of death for many movie vampires, and as with the case of Edward, it can be used by a vampire to indirectly commit suicide. Luckily, Bella is able to steal away from Forks, Washington, without Charlie knowing, and she travels to Italy and saves Edward just in the nick of time. It's not that Edward is disintegrating in the sun, but rather that his skin is sparkling and people will see that he is not human, that perhaps he is a vampire. I'm not sure why sparkling indicates that someone is a vampire, but it would attract the attention of humans, who do not sparkle in the sun.

Sometimes, Charlie is overly protective of Bella, for example when he "grounds" her, but sometimes, as when she travels to Italy, he's totally clueless about what she is doing. If I were watching my daughter's every move to the point of "grounding" her, I would probably figure out that she's disappeared and gone to Italy.

THE SUN GOD AND THE VAMPIRE

The sun was, in many cases, a symbol of the gods and goddesses of ancient times. For example, the ancient Egyptians worshiped Ra, sometimes called Re, and he was the patron of the sun, of light, of power, and of the pharaohs.

Ra was associated mainly with the midday sun, which is the hottest sun of the day. Hence, he was most powerful at high noon, which happens to be the time of day when vampires are most vulnerable to the sun's power to destroy them.

For centuries, Ra was the main sun god throughout Egypt,

his worship based somewhat in Heliopolis, the City of the Sun. The sun was thought to be Ra's body or eye. In addition, Ra was king of the gods and creator of all; mankind was created from his sweat and tears. Later, he was known as Amon-Ra, meaning literally, the sun.[1]

Ra's establishment as sun god started growing in the second dynasty and by the fourth, the Egyptians believed that their pharaohs were Sons of Ra, or manifestations of the god on Earth. By the fifth dynasty, the pharaohs were building solar temples, pyramids, and obelisks in his honor, and he was established as a state deity.

Then by the eleventh dynasty, Ra was elevated further into his more monotheistic version, whereby he had created the world for mankind, and it was men who did bad deeds and caused evil things to happen. He had become a Christian-like god at this point, and some followers thought that Ra would punish them in death if they did evil deeds in life.

In the case of vampires, including Edward, who almost commits suicide by standing in the full blast of the high noon sun in Italy, the sun can punish them by death for doing evil deeds in life. In most cases, the sun itself does the killing, while in Edward's case, his skin sparkles and draws attention, and he could be killed just for sparkling in the sun. While in standard vampire lore, the vampires cannot be in the sun at all, Edward, of course, can handle the weak rays of the sun.

The traditional reason why vampires cannot handle *any* sunlight is that the sun indeed represents the presence of God. Evil must remain in the dark.

---

1. For more details about Ra, see *Why Did It Have to Be Snakes?: From Science to the Supernatural, The Many Mysteries of Indiana Jones*, by Lois H. Gresh and Robert Weinberg (New York: John Wiley & Sons, Inc. 2007).

If you happen to hook up with a vampire boyfriend, you might want to get a huge case of SPF 50 lotion. Make sure your guy is slathered in the sun-blocking ointment at all times.

There are human skin diseases, of course, that are inflamed by exposure to sunlight. Usually, these diseases won't kill you, but they'll cause a lot of pain, and if you're not careful, you could die.

First, there's the obvious: sunburn. This is a photosensitivity reaction in the skin that is diminished if a person has increased melanin pigmentation. If you are sunburned too often, you can develop skin cancer, which can indeed kill you. We all like to soak in the sun, and if we're not naturally dark, a nice tanned glow makes us look healthy. When I was a child and teenager, I was in the sun constantly, and in the summer, I always had a very dark tan. As I've grown older, though, my skin can't handle the sun as well. About a year ago, I was thrilled to go to Miami Beach, Florida, on a mini-excursion. I had a brief amount of time alone, during which I managed to escape to the beach. Within two hours, the skin on my stomach had actually blistered from sunburn! I was in acute pain for the next two days, soaking in cold baths and talking to my mother on my cell phone from the tub. Now I am much more careful at the beach, and while I won't go so far as to wear gigantic floppy beach hats and robes and sit under huge umbrellas, I wear SPF 15 or 35 lotion, which is probably what your vampire man should wear even in Forks, Washington.

The sun contains visible light, obviously, as well as infrared radiation, which supplies the warmth and ultraviolet, or UV, radiation. Typically, visible light and infrared radiation do not cause sunburns and do not damage the skin. So Edward is smart to live in Forks, Washington, where he is exposed to weak visible light, and on those days when it's actually semi-warm there, to infrared radiation. Hopefully, he isn't exposed too much in the way of UV radiation, which is what could hurt him.

Ultraviolet radiation comes in three basic flavors: long wave, sunburn, and short wave. The first type, long-wave UV, can give you a tan. It is not filtered out of the atmosphere and is present pretty much all day.

The second type, sunburn UV, does cause sunburn, as its name suggests, and also wrinkles and ages your skin. It can also cause skin cancer and is most intense at high noon. This is not the type of sunlight that any vampire, including Edward Cullen, should be bathed in.

The third type, short-wave UV, also burns skin and causes skin cancer. It's probably not wise for any human or vampire to be exposed to a lot of short-wave UV.

If UV radiation hits the skin, some of the radiation scatters into the tissues under the skin's surface and is absorbed by the cells. The cell damage causes sunburn, skin cancer, and skin aging.

If someone is taking certain drugs and is exposed to sunlight, he can develop conditions known as phototoxicity and photoallergy. It's possible that most vampires have elements in their blood and tissue that are similar to these human drugs. We do know that the vampire's blood differs from ours. The human drugs that cause the phototoxicity and photoallergy conditions are carried to the skin by the bloodstream. Phototoxic reactions can include serious blisters on the skin and strange pigmentations. In some cases, phototoxicity causes fingernails to peel off!

Photoallergic reactions occur when the body's immune system responds to the combination of sunlight and particular chemicals. The skin often looks as if it has poison ivy.

More serious sunlight diseases include something called solar urticaria, in which the skin erupts with hideous lesions immediately upon exposure to the sun.

The important thing to remember is that even vampires who walk around during the day are affected by intense UV radiation. So keep your vampire guy inside at noon, and never have an argument when the sun is beating down its strongest rays. If anything, when it's noon, give your guy a cold drink, make him shut his eyes, play some soothing, dreamy music, and let him literally chill out until the sun subsides.

Now let's switch gears and explore another traditional icon of the vampire: the cross. The appearance of crosses doesn't seem to bother Edward. He does go to Italy for a long time, and there are cathedrals and churches everywhere in Italy. You cannot get away from crosses in Italy. So for a traditional cross-fearing vampire, Italy doesn't make a great destination or home.

Of course, the Volturi vampires actually live in Volterra, Italy. These vampires rule the underworld and hire other vampires to do their dirty work for them. They've been around for thousands of years, and in *Eclipse*, they come to Forks to destroy Victoria's evil young vampires. The crosses in Volterra don't seem to bother the Volturi vampires, any more than they bother Edward.

As with Forks, Washington, there is also a real place called Volterra, Italy. It's in Tuscany in the province of Pisa. It was settled during the Stone Age and served as a bishop's residence in the fifth century. An ancient city, Volterra has a Roman theater from the year 1 B.C., the beautiful Palazzo dei Priori, and many medieval cathedrals and chapels.

For most vampires, the crucifix is a symbol of death. It is a Latin cross that serves as an iconic representation of Christianity. Jesus Christ was nailed to a cross and died there on Good Friday.

In Eastern Europe, peasants held up crosses, nailed them to

doors, and wore them around their necks to ward off evil. They believed that the crosses held the power of God in them.

But as with Edward Cullen and his vampire family, not all vampires have been afraid of crosses. Anne Rice's Louis, for example, is not frightened away if someone holds up a cross in front of his face. Louis actually enjoys looking at crosses. However, in Anne Rice's novels, the vampires realize that, when they see crosses nailed to doors, it means that the people in that area believe that vampires may be around. Fearing discovery rather than the crosses themselves, Rice's vampires may avoid those areas.

If you fall in love with a vampire who does not fear crosses, consider yourself lucky. You can walk down the street with him without avoiding churches or women wearing crosses around their necks. If your mother wears a cross, you can actually visit her with your guy without worrying that he's going to cringe, hide his face, or worse, disappear in a poof of dust.

But if you fall in love with a traditional vampire who is terrified of crosses, then you have a lot more about which to worry. You won't be able to go many places together, unless of course, you move to the middle of a jungle or to a country where Christianity isn't prevalent. You might be safe in a Buddhist country, for example, where the appearance of a Buddha statue isn't going to maim or kill your man.

In the Twilight Saga, there is no mention of two other traditional items that terrify most vampires: garlic and holy water. Edward is immune to both of these traditional vampire curses, as well as being almost immune to the sun and totally immune to crosses.

In almost all vampire literature and movies, garlic is used by peasants to ward off vampires. In ancient times, the Christian peasants believed that Moslem corpses were the most susceptible to turning into vampires and then killing people. This sprang from the Moslem belief that, as Satan left the Garden of Eden, his footprints left behind tracks of garlic that popped out of the ground he walked on. Hence, the ancient Moslems disliked garlic and viewed it as a symbol of evil. That a symbol of evil wards off an evil vampire is an odd notion. The sun as a symbol of God and purity makes sense as a vampire repellant. Anything that represents good makes sense as a vampire repellant: sun, crosses, holy water; but a symbol of evil, such as garlic, is a bit illogical.

The logic comes from a different use of garlic coupled with the peasant belief about garlic and Satan just described. Throughout the world, people have also used garlic as a medicine and purification tool. Because garlic healed people, so the story went, it was a symbol of good and purity. So it made sense to hang garlic on doorways to ward off evil.

GARLIC

Garlic is in the onion family called Alliaceae and is related to leeks and shallots as well as to the obvious onions. A garlic bulb has many sections called cloves, and to cook the garlic, you peel the coverings off the cloves, grind up the fleshy cloves into tiny bits, add spices, and then fry or otherwise cook the bits and spices until they are basically combined into a thick sauce.

To maintain the freshness and usability of garlic, it is often hung, and sometimes, it is braided and then hung. Hanging the garlic helps to keep it dry. It also wards off any evil spirits that might be lurking in the kitchen. And you never know when an evil spirit is going to infect your food with disease.

In ancient times, garlic was used to cure many diseases, whether inflicted by vampires or by other, more natural causes. It was thought to help patients suffering from maladies as diverse as smallpox and tuberculosis, cancer and heart disease, diabetes and gangrene, and even sun exhaustion and the common cold.

Of course, eating garlic isn't going to cure one common malady, that of halitosis, or bad breath. And to tell the truth, it's probably not going to cure cancer, the common cold, or heart disease, either.

Garlic was so common as a tool to protect people from vampires that in ancient cultures, if a person was allergic to garlic, he might be condemned for *being* a vampire. The habit of testing a person for vampirism using garlic was used in Slavic countries, and in Romania, South America, China, and Mexico.

It was common practice to hand out garlic at church just to make sure no vampires were present. After all, you can never have enough protection from evil. If the Sunday morning sunlight doesn't kill the vampire as he walks into the church, if the crosses hanging all over the place don't kill him, if the holy water doesn't fry him into a crisp, then handing out garlic might do the trick.

Even if your vampire guy is like Edward and does not recoil in terror when he's around garlic, it might be wise, just as a precaution, to avoid cooking with garlic or having it hanging in braids on the kitchen door. It's not much to give up for your man.

As for holy water, most people don't have urns of the stuff in their bedrooms and kitchens. Most holy water is found in Roman Catholic, Eastern Orthodox, Anglican, and other churches, and in tiny bottles that priests carry for specific purposes (exorcisms come to mind). Hence, you probably don't have to worry about taking any precautions when it comes to holy water. Besides, a vampire such as Edward is immune to holy water, just as he's immune to the other common vampire repellants.

Holy water is ordinary water that has been blessed by a priest, who may then use the water for baptisms and other blessings, oh and also for exorcisms, of course. The holy water is kept near the entrance of the church to remind people when they come to pray that they have been baptized into the Christian faith. In Roman Catholic churches, some people dip their fingers into the holy water and then do the sign of the cross, a double killer-whammy for traditional vampires.

After being used, where does holy water go? Can you dispose of holy water by flushing it down a regular sink into your regular plumbing? Absolutely not, as you may have guessed. Because it is holy, blessed by God, the water must be drained directly into the ground. This makes some sense, I suppose, except that it might make *more* sense to let the used holy water evaporate up into heaven.

EXORCISM AND VAMPIRES

Typically, vampires are immune to exorcisms by priests. Because they are born by being infected by the blood of an existing vampire, the creatures are physically transformed into vampires. They are not transformed because evil spirits are wandering around seeking new bodies to inhabit and decide that their bodies will do. With exorcisms, it is the evil spirits that are exhumed from the living human bodies they inhabit.

However, there are times when exorcisms are performed on vampires. For example, in the 1992 film *Bram Stoker's Dracula*, Anthony Hopkins plays Dr. Van Helsing, who operates as an exorcist of vampirism in the tradition of exorcists in movies such as the 1973 film *The Exorcist*. Anthony Hopkins is out to purge Dracula's evil spirit from the bodies of vampires, whereas in *The Exorcist*, the priest was out to purge demonic evil spirits from the body of a young, innocent girl.

In the case of *The Exorcist*, one of the most popular horror films of all time, a real shocker when it was released, the possession by demons of twelve-year-old actress Linda Blair was based on a real two-month-long exorcism performed by Jesuit priest Friar William S. Bowdern. A fourteen-year-old boy was supposedly possessed by demons in the real version of the story.

Linda Blair's character is cleansed of demons by a series of Latin prayers, continual dousing in holy water, and the thrusting of gigantic crosses at her. The film was followed by countless exorcism movies, such as the Omen trilogy, in which a little boy is possessed by demons and requires exorcism.

In 1992's *Bram Stoker's Dracula*, Dr. Van Helsing does many of the same things that the priest does in *The Exorcist*. He constantly chants Latin prayers, sprinkles holy water, and thrusts gigantic crosses at the vampires. When Lucy is transformed into a vampire and shows up in a crypt carrying a whimpering child, Van Helsing holds up a giant cross, and she recoils in terror. Then as Van Helsing starts screaming exorcism prayers, Lucy vomits blood at him, just as Linda Blair's character vomited at her priest during exorcisms.

(continued)

Later, when Dracula comes as a green fog to Renfield's cell in the mental institution, we see Dr. Van Helsing once again chanting exorcism prayers and sprinkling holy water. The exorcism component of this film is so similar to the movie with Linda Blair that Van Helsing is constantly chanting, "Christ compels you," a line made famous in *The Exorcist* as "The power of Christ compels you." He drives away Dracula's three vampire wives by chanting exorcism prayers "in the name of Christ."

The 1992 film was terrific, though I must admit that the portrayal of Van Helsing as an exorcist amused me. It seemed contrived and much too "borrowed" from *The Exorcist*. Anthony Hopkins, of course, is an intense and excellent actor, and he pulled off the role of Van Helsing well. But I couldn't buy into the notion of Van Helsing as an exorcist of demonic spirits. Vampires aren't possessed by demons. They are evil entities unto themselves; they are bitten by other vampires and born into vampirism.

Imagine how silly it would be if a character in Twilight tried to exorcise demonic spirits from Edward Cullen. He would probably laugh and simply walk away.

CHAPTER 14

PROTECTING YOUR VAMPIRE, PART 2:

Everything You Need to Know About Coffins, Black Capes, Bats, Wooden Stakes Through the Heart, Decapitation, and Fire

✧

Edward Cullen does not need any sleep. He does not need a bed, and he does not need a coffin like most vampires. He tells Bella Swan that the notion of vampires sleeping all day in coffins is pure myth.

Which would you prefer, a boyfriend who sleeps in a coffin all day, or a boyfriend who watches *you* sleep all night? It's a tough choice.

Traditionally, vampires sleep in coffins because they are considered to be the living dead. When a vampire moves to a new location, such as across an ocean from Transylvania to London, he brings the coffin with him. In fact, he must bring his own coffin, not another vampire's coffin or any old corpse's coffin, and the coffin must contain dirt from the vampire's homeland.

This could make for some complications. For example, consider if, after three hundred years, the vampire's coffin finally rots away. It is, after all, made out of pine or some other form of wood, and wood does not necessarily last forever. So the coffin rots, and our vampire is left without a bed. According to folk tradition, he's not allowed to sleep in another vampire's coffin or in a dead guy's coffin. Of course, Dracula and Nosferatu both have many coffins (or crates resembling coffins) with them on their journey across the sea. So perhaps if a vampire owns multiple "beds," he can use any of them rather than his original crypt.

As for the homeland dirt, what happens if the ship sinks at sea before reaching London? All the homeland dirt is lost in the ocean, along with the special coffins and crates. What does our vampire do then? If a vampire doesn't have a coffin as a bed, can he sleep at all? And if a vampire doesn't get enough sleep, does he become even more creepy and dangerous? Given that vampires are already pretty vile guys (except for special cases, as with Edward Cullen, when they are "nice" vampires), an exhausted vampire could be extremely dangerous.

If the ship reaches its destination without losing the vampire's homeland soil, the vampire then hires ratlike moronic guys to lug his coffins of soil to his new castlelike home. He must choose ratlike moronic guys because anyone else might guess quite easily that a creepy-looking fellow with no suitcase but say, fifty heavy coffins of dirt happens to be a vampire.

It remains a mystery how villagers and people in London don't notice brutes lugging dozens of heavy dirt-filled coffins through the streets. Even if it's done in the dead of night, people are going to notice a procession of this kind. I live in a small village, and if at midnight, former prison inmates were hauling fifty coffins down my street, if I didn't happen to notice them, I am sure that one or more of my neighbors would. I have to give credit to Stoker's Dracula, who had the thugs place his crates of lucky vampire dirt all over London in various remote locations. In this way, should someone discover the crates in one location, Dracula could quickly move somewhere else. The novel does indeed have pursuers locate the crates and destroy them, but by the time they get close enough to the final crate, Dracula escapes.

At any rate, in general vampire tales, the coffins arrive at the vampire's new place of residence, where the thugs haul them down to the basement. To regenerate his strength, supposedly, the vampire must be in his coffin, or at least with some of that homeland dirt on him. This typical vampire folds his arms over his chest, shuts his eyes, and (very dramatically) sits in the coffin and then lowers himself rigidly down until his head is resting on the dirt. The lid of the coffin closes.

Keep in mind that this typical vampire (not a member of the Cullen family, of course, since they do not have to sleep at all), goes to sleep every night wearing an ankle-length, unwrinkled, perfectly clean black cape, usually a pristine shirt and black pants, perfectly ironed and creased. His hair is neatly combed, and his face is typically shaven. (In the case of Nosferatu, aka Count Orlock, he sometimes ignores the entire routine and just hangs upside down like a gigantic bat-human to sleep. And with Nosferatu, of course, he never looks good, whether he's awake or asleep.)

We never see the vampire shave, yet he's always free of stubble on his face. Perhaps the aging process stops at seventeen (or whatever real age the vampire is when he's transformed from human into vampire), leaving all hair and whiskers at the same length for the rest of eternity.

We never see a vampire comb his hair, either, though typically, vampires have incredibly gorgeous and perfect hair. But at some point, he's going to have to groom himself because, folks: he sleeps in dirt every single night!

If you slept in a coffin of dirt, then when you awakened, the hair on the back of your head would be coated or at least dusted heavily in dirt. The back of all of your clothing would also be coated in dirt. I assume that vampires don't sweat because they are described as so cold all the time. Any sweat, or even moisture from the damp basements, would tend to cake the dirt on the vampires' hair and bodies. Dirt plus moisture equals mud.

So how do you think the vampire wakes up and automatically is still wearing a clean, perfectly ironed cape with a clean pair of ironed pants, and how does he have perfectly clean hair, and so forth? Perhaps the rats lick him at night. Or perhaps vampire clothing just never gets dirty. It's made from special cloth that repels all dirt and moisture. After all, the vampire seems to wear the same outfit every day and every night, he does not wash his clothes, and he never travels with spare capes and so forth.

It's rather refreshing that Stephenie Meyer chose to omit the coffin and soil routine for her vampires. It would be much harder to believe that Bella Swan would fall in love with a caped vampire coated in dirt every day during biology class. It's much easier to believe that she falls in love with a clean-cut vampire who wears normal clothes and doesn't reek of musty, moldy, damp dirt.

The whole notion of vampires and coffins is much over-played. In reality, people believed in vampires before people used coffins to bury the dead. In the time when Carlisle Cullen turned into a vampire, for example, only wealthy people in real life could afford to be buried in coffins. Although Carlisle appears to be twenty-three years old, he was born in the 1640s and died in the 1660s.

As an aside, Peter Facinelli, who plays the role of Carlisle Cullen in the Twilight movie, is in reality thirty-four years old and married to the actress Jennie Garth, who became extremely famous for playing the role of Kelly Taylor in *Beverly Hills, 90210*. A high school character, Kelly was much more screwed up than, say, Bella Swan, who goes so far as to try to kill herself in *New Moon*.

Kelly had trouble with boys; falling in love too easily with both main male characters in her television program, she suffered from a miscarriage, she was raped and shot. If that wasn't enough, Kelly abused drugs, got amnesia, and even joined a cult. Of course, she didn't do all of these things at the same time. Her ordeals were spread out over the course of the long-playing and very popular program. Anyway, Peter Facinelli and Jennie Garth have three daughters: real children, unlike Facinelli's character in *Twilight*. Of interest, his oldest daughter, born in 1997 and long before the Twilight movie, is named Luca *Bella*.

So in Carlisle Cullen's time, unless he was fabulously wealthy when he died, there would not have been a coffin for him. Back then, dead people were wrapped in burial shrouds and placed underground. Animals could easily dig up corpses that were buried in shallow graves.

By the early eighteenth century, more of the common people were buried in coffins. Just in case the newly deceased person happened to be a vampire, a stake was driven through its heart before burial. Sometimes, even more gruesome, people would nail the clothes and even the arms and legs of the corpse to the coffin itself. It was believed that this secured the would-be vampire in place inside the coffin so he could not roam the villages and suck blood. Also, many people believed that vampires still confined in coffins beneath the ground would eat their own arms and legs before they escaped to roam and suck blood. Thus, the coffin was actually necessary to trap the vampire in place, and hopefully, let him gnaw his own arms and legs off.

Of course, people also believed that vampires were shapeshifters, meaning they could transform into wolves, bats, and even mist, among other entities. Thus, even inside the coffin with his clothes nailed to the wood, a vampire could shapeshift into, say, mist and then escape through a hole in the ground and go on his bloody rampage all night. Securing the vampire to the coffin doesn't make much sense after you factor in the shapeshifting skills.

In fiction, the very early vampires, such as Lord Ruthven and Varney the Vampire, did not have coffins. They rested when they were tired, but didn't seem to need special places for sleeping.

Bram Stoker's Dracula (the vampire in the book version) also did not have a coffin for sleeping, but he did need the homeland dirt in order to get a good day's rest. So he brought crates, which looked a bit like coffins, with him across the ocean, and the crates were filled with dirt. When the homeland special dirt became "soiled" by religious objects, Dracula had to return to Transylvania. In fact, Van Helsing puts Eucharistic wafers into a tomb marked "Dracula" at the end of the novel, hence making sure Dracula cannot return to sleep there.

Although Dracula, in the original Stoker version, did not have a real coffin, the 1931 Bela Lugosi Dracula does have a coffin. In the film, Dracula's wives also sleep in coffins.

We know that Edward and the other members of his family can survive in the weak sunlight of Forks, Washington. We also know that they don't require sleep. So they have no need for coffins at all. But if they were susceptible to damage by the sunlight and needed some rest, a coffin would make sense. With the lid down, the vampire isn't exposed to any damaging sunlight, and he's well protected from enemies who might expose him while he's sleeping.

In fact, in Anne Rice's Vampire Chronicles series of novels, vampires sleep in coffins to shield themselves from the sun. In one amusing twist in Rice's *Interview with the Vampire*, Lestat de Lioncourt transforms Louis into a vampire but forgets to obtain a coffin for the new vampire. Given that day was imminent, the two vampires, old and new, sleep together in Lestat's coffin.

Clearly, if your vampire guy is like Edward and does not sleep in a coffin, you need not protect him from those who search for vampire coffins and homeland dirt. In fact, if you're smart, you might want to place fifty "fake" vampire coffins filled with ordinary dirt all over town. When the vampire hunters suspect your man of being a vampire, they'll search everywhere for his coffin, they'll destroy all of the fifty fake ones, and they'll *still* never find him. This is a very good bluffing technique, which I highly recommend if you want to protect your Edward-like guy.

If your vampire man is more typical and needs his coffins and dirt, then perhaps you can both live next to a huge cemetery. Nobody will ever be able to figure out which coffin he's living in during the day.

As for the black capes, as mentioned earlier, it's lucky for Edward and Bella's romance that he doesn't wear one. He'd look pretty freaky at school wearing an ordinary vampire getup. Girls wouldn't find him particularly attractive.

The black of the cape, of course, symbolizes death and night. It is the absence of color. It is shadow. A vampire attired in black blends in with the night. If he were wearing peacock blue or neon green, he'd really stick out at night. If he tried to slither across the lawn or up the side of your house, dressed in green-and-red plaid suits, you and other people would be much more likely to notice him.

In general, being a vampire could get pretty boring after several hundred years of wearing nothing but black. These undead are not particularly known as trendy fashionistas. In fact, the overall Goth look has been around for so long that it's no longer cool. I hate to think of the number of cows sacrificed in the name of black clothing coolness. Ten or twenty years ago, everyone wore black clothes all the time, thinking it was an ultra-cool look. Everyone, even businesspeople, wore black leather jackets and black pants. They wore so many pairs of black pants and so many black shirts that, walking through any modern city during the work week was like walking through a sea of morticians. Punk Goths were everywhere, a fashion that began as far back as the seventies. But today, you have to be a true Goth to take on the Goth look. It's no longer all that unusual a look.

For now, let's return to the notion of black capes, something that the Cullen family does without. While traditional vampires liked their capes, more modern vampires tend to be like the Cullen clan: they wear normal clothes. This enables them to fit in very easily in any city or town without being noticed. If a guy's walking down the streets of New York City donned in a vampire's black cape, he's going to be noticed, but if the same guy's wearing jeans and a T-shirt, nobody will assume he's a vampire (or a Goth wanting to look like a real, no-cape vampire).

So the vampire of modern times has returned to his roots, because prior to Bela Lugosi's Dracula, vampires of ancient folklore didn't wear Victorian British society evening clothes and black opera capes. It was Hamilton Deane, a writer for the theater, who first portrayed Dracula as wearing evening clothes and the opera cape. But it was Bela Lugosi who truly made Dracula immortal with his sophisticated demeanor, the sexy voice, the black slicked-back hair, the intense eyes, and the black opera cape.

Bram Stoker's Dracula (the vampire in the book version) wore black clothes but no cape, had black hair and a thick moustache, and had blue eyes that flashed red when he was upset. He was older, such as Bela Lugosi, rather than young like Edward Cullen, but as the novel progressed, he became younger and younger.

As for protecting your vampire man, if he wears a black cape, hide it from him and never let him wear it again. It marks him clearly as a vampire. If he argues with you that he absolutely must have the cape back, tell him you lost it and you don't have any idea where it is.

Another clue to people that you are with a vampire man is that bats may follow you around all the time. If your neighbor sees a huge bat flying into your bedroom at dawn and leaving at nightfall, he might guess that you're living with a vampire. If flocks of bats congregate around only your house, then it's a clear indication that you have something creepy going on around you, that maybe, just maybe, you are hosting a vampire or two. And obviously, if fifty vampires leave your house, attack the village priest, then return, only to leave the next night and attack the town children, your neighbors will *know* that you are implicated. Your vampire guy will be uncovered.

Bats are typically associated with vampires because one type of bat, the vampire bat, sucks blood. It was Bram Stoker who tied the bat to Dracula in his 1897 novel. Dracula was able to summon and rule creatures of the night, including the bat, and Dracula was also able to transform himself into a bat, among other shapes. Very early in *Dracula*, a bat shows up outside Jonathan Harker's window in Dracula's castle, and later, Harker sees Dracula crawling like a bat down the outside of the castle walls. In London, Dracula often assumes bat form to traverse the city quickly without being noticed.

Ever since Bram Stoker's *Dracula*, bats and vampires have been inseparable. But sometimes, as with the Twilight vampires, they don't play any role at all.

THE VAMPIRE BAT

Vampire bats live in Mexico, South America, and Central America. There are only three species of vampire bats out of almost one thousand species of bats, overall. The vampire bats are in the mammalian family of Phyllostomatidae and subfamily of Desmodontinae, with the most common vampire bat being *Desmodus rotundus*, and the other two being *Diaemus youngi* and *Diphylla ecaudata*. Of all the mammals, only bats are able to fly.

Bats are similar to cats in that they sleep most of the time. Other than that, they probably don't have much in common with cats. For one thing, your cat will be furious at you and claw your eyes out if you try to force him to sleep upside down. The bat prefers the upside-down sleeping position so it can drop off its perch and fly quickly away.

Most bats eat fruits and insects. Vampire bats obviously drink blood. And they typically don't eat anything other than blood. They are indeed like vampires.

Desmodus rotundus, the common vampire bat, only drinks the blood of other mammals. The rarer vampire bats, *Diaemus youngi* and *Diphylla ecaudata*, drink blood from birds. Notice I didn't use the phrase *suck blood*, and that's because vampire bats, unlike their human vampire counterparts, don't really suck the blood from their prey. Instead, a vampire bat uses heat sensors to find a vein in its prey, sinks its razorlike teeth into the vein, then when the blood is flowing freely, say from a thick vein in your neck, the vampire bat just laps it up. This is something else that the vampire bat has in common with your cat. While the cat laps up milk and water using its tongue, the vampire bat laps up your blood using its tongue. I don't know about you, but I think the cat makes a better pet.

To keep your blood from clotting while they're lapping you dry, the vampire bat's saliva has an anticoagulant ingredient. When the bat has slurped you dry and fallen off your neck from being bloated with all your blood, the cuts in your neck start scabbing into what look like vampire puncture wounds. The vampire bat actually drinks approximately fifteen milliliters of blood at a given feeding, which doesn't sound like much until you realize that fifteen milliliters is between 40 and 50 percent of the bat's weight before it started drinking you dry. This is why the vampire bat becomes so bloated after each meal. Oddly, in the movies, we never see vampires who gain tons of weight and look bloated after a neck feeding. They remain trim and slim at all times. But real vampire bats get so swollen with your blood that they cannot even leave and go home until their bodies have digested most of the meal.

Most likely, vampires, possibly even Edward Cullen, must possess some form of anticoagulant in their saliva to keep blood flowing as they feed. Most blood-sucking insects, such as mosquitoes, also slobber anticoagulants onto their victims.

Most vampires, including Edward, enjoy their sense of smell. Edward explains to Bella that he breathes, not because he *has* to breathe but because it gives him the much enjoyed sense of smell. He often knows where she is because he can smell her scent from far away.

Vampire bats also have a keen sense of smell, but they actually identify their prey by the sounds of breathing. According

(continued)

to *Science Daily,* "Vampire bats feed on the same prey over several nights and the authors of the study [Udo Groeger and Lutz Wiegrebe from the Ludwig-Maximilians-Universitaet in Munich, Germany] propose that the bats use breathing sounds to identify their prey in the same way as humans use voice to recognize one another."[1]

In addition, the vampire bat is very athletic, and not only does it fly, it has strong legs and can crawl, hop, jump, walk, and run, whereas not all bat species perform these amazing feats of strength and agility. Again, this has some similarity to the human vampire, which is always portrayed as being a superathlete. Although it is small, usually about the size of a human thumb with a wingspan of eight inches, the vampire bat is the superathlete of the bat world.

Unlike human vampires, the vampire bat isn't really all that attracted to human blood. In fact, the bat prefers animal blood to human blood. However, when farm animals and other beasts aren't available, the vampire bat will attack humans.

But do they go for the neck?

Oddly enough, the answer is *no.* While "to the bats, a sleeping human is just another large, warm and unconscious animal . . .They're more likely to go for a person's big toe," Barbara French, a bat expert at Bat Conservation International, a Texas-based nonprofit organization, told *Live Science* magazine. "There's a good blood supply there and the bite is usually less noticeable."[2]

---

1. "Vampire Bats Recognize Their Prey's Breathing," *Science Daily,* June 16, 2006, at http://www.sciencedaily.com/releases/2006/06/060616124642.htm.
2. Ker Than, "Behind the Recent Spate of Vampire Bat Attacks," *Live Science,* November 14, 2005, at http://www.livescience.com/animals/051104_vampire-_bats.html.

Having a vampire dude like gorgeous Edward Cullen sucking your big toe isn't nearly as sexy as having him nibbling on your neck. But facts are facts, girls. Of course, there are differences between vampire bats and human vampires, so we can allow that while vampire bats suck on your toes, vampire dudes prefer to nibble on your neck.

A very distinct threat to your vampire man is any clan such as Twilight's Volturi coven. The royal vampire clan, they are so powerful and rule so many strong vampires that they have the ability to execute other vampires.

We know that vampires can die in the Twilight Saga. They kill each other, often. In *Eclipse*, Stephenie Meyer tells us that vampires fought very fierce battles a long time ago, killing each other, and that the Volturi try to keep things under control. We're told that newborn vampires are wild, unpredictable, and extremely capable of killing other vampires, especially when the young ones attack in groups. Jasper, for example, was a trained vampire fighter for a long time until he simply grew tired of killing other vampires and wanted a more peaceful existence.

Another clue is found in *Eclipse*, when Edward disposes of Victoria. Here, the fighting seems the same as between mortal humans, except of course, the vampires move like flashes of lightning and have more strength and power than a thousand grizzly bears. But Victoria is a vampire who wants to kill Bella Swan, and Edward must intervene. He kills Victoria in a match of sheer strength, then his mouth brushes her neck as if in a vampire kiss of death. She is ripped into pieces and burned.

Those are just two clues about how vampires are killed in the

Twilight series. There are many more methods, but the common way is to rip the vampire to shreds and burn him or her.

For most vampires, death comes by a stake through the heart, decapitation, and setting the body on fire. Twilight departs with the usual methods, except for setting the body on fire, which seems to be a necessary part of the death ritual of Twilight vampires.

Long ago, in Sheridan Le Fanu's short story "Carmilla," the stake was a remedy to vampirism, and it's been around ever since. A stake through the heart was an ancient vampire remedy, going back through time even before humans buried our dead in coffins. Remember what we said about nailing suspected vampires into their coffins? This is why people long ago began driving stakes through the hearts of suspected vampires, to nail them to the ground so they couldn't get loose and run amuck, killing people and terrorizing villages and towns. Sometimes the stake was driven through the stomach instead of the heart, because again, the original purpose of staking the vampire was to secure him to the ground.

Various types of stakes were used to "kill" vampires, such as ones made from iron as well as from wood. The types of stakes varied from region to region, and in some places, specific woods were used, such as juniper, ash, or hawthorn.

The practice of using hawthorn wood to ward off supernatural evil in the form of witches and sorcerers stretches back as far as ancient Greece. In particular, wood from the hawthorn tree was popular throughout southern Europe and represented protection against all forms of supernatural evil, including vampirism. Hawthorn chips and bark were put in the cradles of babies and by the beds of children, and arrayed around entrances to houses and churches. It was thought that the wood not only blocked evil forces, it also was sacred and represented holiness, which definitely is not favored by vampires and other demonic entities. People generally believed that Jesus Christ wore a crown of thorns made in part by the hawthorn tree. Hence, it was sacred stuff, and just like Van Helsing's Eucharist wafer placed inside the "DRACULA" tomb, a stake made from hawthorn wood would destroy any vampire. In fact, Van Helsing claimed that putting wood from the wild rose bush on a coffin would ensure that any vampire contained inside would not be able to get out. The hawthorn is a rose tree and is also called by various other names such as the wild rose and the black thorn.

While stakes were driven through stomachs and even backs of supposed vampires, when people started using coffins to bury the dead, the stakes had to be driven through the heart. It no longer sufficed to nail the corpse to the ground. Now the vampire killer had to drive the stake through the part of the body representing the blood: the heart.

As for decapitation, it, too, is a common method of disposing of pesky vampires. In Bram Stoker's *Dracula*, Dr. Van Helsing had to prove to Lucy Westenra's fiancé, Arthur Holmwood, that she was truly a vampire before Holmwood would allow the decapitation. In older times, people thought that without a head, a person's body would be soulless. So if Lucy was dead but still a human being rather than a vampire, she had to retain her soul in the afterlife. If Lucy was a vampire, she already had no soul, and Arthur Holmwood could agree to the decapitation without worrying that he was keeping his beloved Lucy out of heaven.

It's possible that decapitation as a method of vampire destruction is similar to the notion of nailing the vampire's arms and legs to his coffin. There's not much a vampire can do without his head. If he's a modern vampire *and* a doctor like Dr. Carlisle

Cullen, then it's possible he could rise from the coffin and then perform surgery on himself, reattaching his own head.

But that's a stretch, to put it mildly. Let's assume that the medical doctor vampire is extremely strong and just rips his arms and legs from the nails securing them to the coffin. He has no head. He fumbles around in the coffin, finds his head buried at his feet, and grabs it. He transforms into mist and escapes from the grave through a hole in the ground, still grasping his detached head. As mist, he makes his way to the funeral home or nearby hospital, where surgical equipment is available. He slithers down the hall after everyone has gone home, or in the case of a busy hospital, he slinks into the operating room while someone is giving birth.

Choosing an operating room where someone is having brain surgery or heart surgery wouldn't make sense. During those procedures, the doctors and nurses are keenly aware of everything that's happening with their surgical tools, or so we hope. In the room where the baby is being born, the mother is wailing and totally out of it; the father, if he's even present, has already fainted and is on the floor; the nurses are oohing and aahing over the baby and rushing the newborn to safety; the doctor is probably making golf arrangements on his cell phone or racing from the room to deliver another baby somewhere else. If you were a medical-doctor vampire in need of surgical equipment, wouldn't you choose a birthing room rather than a heart operating room where everyone is keenly focused on everything and precisely aware of the locations of all surgical clamps, scalpels, and so forth?

So our guy slips as mist into the room where the baby is being born. Still as mist, he swipes some surgical needles and thread, clamps, and so on, from a nearby table. The mother screams, the father faints. Nobody notices the mist at the back of the room. But the vampire still has a problem. Sure, he has the necessary equipment, but he's *headless*. How is he supposed to think and hence remember or figure out how to sew his own head back on? How can he see to know what he's doing with the needles and scalpels?

In fact, from this example, you can easily figure out why decapitation was used to destroy vampires. It kept the vampire's head (brain, eyes, etc.) from directing the vampire around town. A headless vampire is pretty worthless.

Edward Cullen's method of ripping his vampire prey into pieces probably has the same purpose as decapitation. A vampire who is in two hundred pieces is going to have a hard time wandering around town and causing problems.

Because many people believed that even a sliver of the vampire's body could recreate the entire creature, in old times, not only were vampires decapitated, they were burned just as Edward burns his vampire prey. In many folklore tales, not only were vampires staked through the heart, nailed into their coffins, beheaded, doused with holy water, and buried with garlic, many were cut into pieces and burned into ashes, and even then, the ashes were scattered lest the vampire be able to resurrect himself with them.

In ancient times, fire was one of the many symbols of the gods. Remember, the sun itself was considered a god in many cultures, as we discussed earlier in this book. Fire would cleanse the world of the vampire. In Christian societies, such as small villages in Eastern Europe, people knew that the Bible used fire to represent God's cleansing the Earth of evil. For example, God uses fire to destroy the evil cities of Sodom and Gomorrah, and in Revelations, God cleanses the entire Earth with fire at the end of all time. In the Bible, fire destroys and cleans, leaving what's left behind pure.

Throughout Eastern Europe, fire was used to destroy all remnants of the staked, decapitated, hacked-into-pieces vampire. Fire was also used to kill diseased animals and even entire villages that might be contaminated.

In literature, fire is used all the time to kill vampires. Indeed, Varney the Vampire actually jumped into a volcano! Anne Rice's vampires had to be burned to be destroyed, and the vampire Magnus actually commits suicide by leaping into the flames. Throughout Anne Rice's novels, vampires use fire against one another, for example, burning the Theatre of the Vampires to the ground in Paris to rid the city of vampires. St. Germain in Chelsea Quinn Yarbro's vampire novels also knows that fire is the one method that definitely destroys vampire enemies.

If your man is a vampire who is somewhat like Edward, you may not have to worry too much about weak sunlight, garlic, and holy water, but definitely, watch his head at all times and do not let anyone play with fire around him. Here are some pointers to keep in mind:

1. Remove all axes from the house, just in case an intruder wants to behead your man.
2. Never use huge butcher knives in the kitchen. They can be used to rip your man into shreds.
3. Do not roast marshmallows and make S'mores with your man.
4. Do not cook hotdogs over a campfire.
5. Definitely make sure that you do not buy a house with fireplaces.
6. Do not keep any matches in the house, not for any reason.

The best way to protect your vampire man from any harm is to somehow become an extremely powerful vampire goddess. This way, you can protect each other. If a vampire like Victoria shows up and almost kills your guy, you can step into action and beat her off. You won't even need hotdogs, marshmallows, or S'mores, because you'll only be lusting for blood, but what the heck, that's a small price to pay for keeping your lover safe.

VAMPIRE TEST!

✦

Earlier in the book, I gave you a vampire quiz. By now, heading into Chapter 15, you must be an expert on the subject. Test your knowledge about vampires and find out if you have what it takes to become one or find one. As usual, after the questions, I'll tell you how to score your answers.

Question #1. Who was the author of the female vampire tale called "Carmilla"?
  A. Bram Stoker
  B. Stephenie Meyer
  C. Bella Swan
  D. Rosalie Cullen
  E. J. S. Le Fanu
  F. H. P. Lovecraft
  G. Charles Dickens
  H. Edward Allan Poe

Question #2. What was the name of the lead vampire in Stephen King's *Salem's Lot*?

A. Stephen King
B. Montague Summers
C. Count Germaine
D. Carmilla
E. Edward Cullen
F. Bella Swan
G. Richard Straker
H. Yo Mama
I. J. S. Le Fanu
J. Bram Stoker

Question #3. In traditional vampire folklore, there are numerous ways to kill a vampire. Which of these methods were not valid ways of destroying a vampire? (Note: More than one answer is correct.)
A. Drowning in the bathtub
B. Choking on a chicken bone
C. Pouring gasoline on the body
D. Burying the body in a cardboard box in the cemetery
E. Decapitating the vampire
F. Burning the vampire
G. Driving a stake through the vampire's heart
H. Exposing the vampire to bright sunlight
I. Forcing the vampire to marry your grandma
J. Making the vampire learn Latin and ancient Greek

Question #4. Who wrote novels about the vampire, the Count of Saint Germain?
A. Stephenie Meyer
B. Anne Rice

C. Yo Mama

D. Chelsea Quinn Yarbro

Question #5. Where does a traditional vampire sleep during the day?

A. He doesn't sleep. Like Edward, he stays up all night and watches *you* sleep.

B. In a coffin filled with homeland dirt

C. In heaven

D. In biology class

E. On a vampiric yacht that goes only to London

F. In his moldy, musty, damp basement on a chaise lounge

G. In Forks, Washington

Question #6. What should you wear around your neck to keep the ordinary vampires away from you?

A. A cross

B. Braided garlic and onions with chili peppers and hot sauce

C. An entire hawthorn tree

D. A Romanian artichoke

E. A photo of Jacob Black

Question #7. What do vampire bats feed on? Choose all answers that are correct.

A. Fruits and insects

B. Dried blood frozen on sticks, also known as bloodsicles

C. Mammalian blood

D. Blood of cows

E. Blood from your neck

F. Blood from your big toes
G. Blood from your veins
H. Caviar and champagne
I. Crêpes with cheese filling and strawberry sauce
J. Ice cream and peanuts
K. Blood
L. More blood
M. And even more blood

Question #8. Which nineteen-year-old actress plays the role of Bella Swan in the Twilight movie?
   A. Jennie Garth
   B. Anne Rice
   C. Kristen Stewart
   D. Stephenie Meyer
   E. Charlene Hale

Question #9. Which English actor plays the role of Edward Cullen in the Twilight movie?
   A. Jack Nicholson
   B. General Patton
   C. Robert Pattinson
   D. Esme Huntington
   E. Brad Pitt

Question #10. What kind of drink does a vampire prefer?
   A. Tap water
   B. Bottled water
   C. Holy water
   D. Grapefruit juice

E. Kool-Aid

F. Blood

Scoring this test is easy. If you have what it takes to become a vampire or to find a vampire, then you need a perfect score. Otherwise, you should probably read more vampire novels and watch more vampire movies, then take the test again. For each question for which you marked down all of the correct answers, give yourself one point. Remember, you need a total score of 10 to succeed on this test.

THE ANSWERS

Question #1. The answer is E, J. S. Le Fanu, the author of the female vampire tale called "Carmilla."

Question #2. The answer is G, Richard Straker, the name of the lead vampire in Stephen King's *Salem's Lot*. This answer should be obvious by a process of elimination. None of the other answers makes any sense. It's possible that you mistakenly guessed the Count of Saint Germaine, but no, that vampire was not in *Salem's Lot*.

Question #3. In traditional folklore, invalid methods of killing a vampire are A, drowning in the bathtub; B, choking on a chicken bone; C, pouring gasoline on the body; D, burying the body in a cardboard box in the cemetery (I truly hope you guessed D!); I, forcing the vampire to marry your grandma (if you did not guess I, give up now and go to summer school for the next ten years); and J, making the vampire learn Latin and ancient Greek. All other methods are valid ways of killing a traditional vampire. Usually, the vampire is killed with a wooden stake, by decapitation, and by sunlight and fire. In Twilight, vampires are ripped into pieces and burned.

Question #4. The answer is D, Chelsea Quinn Yarbro, who wrote novels about the vampire the Count of Saint Germaine. I mentioned the Count of Saint Germaine in Question #2.

Question #5. The answer is B, a traditional vampire sleeps in a coffin filled with homeland dirt during the day. If you were thinking about Edward Cullen, perhaps D, in biology class, would be a close answer.

Question #6. The answer is A, you should wear a cross around your neck to keep the ordinary vampires away from you. The braided garlic would work, but who would want to wear onions with chili peppers and hot sauce around her neck? A cross is much easier.

Question #7. The answers are C, vampire bats feed on mammalian blood; D, blood of cows; E, blood from your neck; F, blood from your big toes; G, blood from your veins; K, blood; L, more blood; and M, even more blood.

Question #8. The answer is C. Kristen Stewart plays the role of Bella Swan in the Twilight movie, and I truly hope you chose the correct answer for this question!

Question #9. The answer is C. Robert Pattinson plays the role of Edward Cullen in the Twilight movie, and as with the previous question, I really hope you got this one right! If not, shame on you!

Question #10. Easy answer! A vampire prefers to drink E, Kool-Aid.

Just kidding. It's not Kool-Aid. It's F, blood! Du-uh!

This was an easy test, and you probably got most, if not all, of the answers right. If you want to fall in love with a vampire, it's very important to know your vampire lore.

CHAPTER 16

LIVING FOREVER:

Is It All That It's Cracked Up to Be?

✧

Many people dream of living forever. Certainly, a lot of people want to remain young and not age, hence the huge market for antiaging cosmetics and surgeries. But there is no fountain of youth, and there is no remedy for ultimate death. We are flesh and blood, creatures of nature, and everything in nature eventually dies.

Or does it?

The animal called the hydra does not age. This is a freshwater animal that mainly lives in streams, lakes, and ponds in warm areas. A hydra is very small, maybe only one to twenty millimeters long. It can regenerate parts of itself that become injured or detached.

The hydra looks like a microscopic tube with an adhesive foot, which is called the basal disc. The creature's mouth is at the other end of its body, a full one to twenty millimeters away from its sticky foot. Half a dozen to a dozen tentacles float around the mouth, and each tentacle is coated with cnidocytes, which are "stinging" cells. When the hydra is near something it might want to eat, the cnidocytes inject the potential food with a hairlike dart of neurotoxins. These neurotoxins paralyze the hydra's prey, typically tiny aquatic invertebrates with glamorous names such as cyclops and daphnia.

The cyclops derives its name from, yes, the ancient Greek Cyclops from mythology, because the little creature appears to have one huge eye. It's hard to imagine a microscopic creature such as a cyclops, that is only a half-millimeter to a few millimeters long, being paralyzed by another animal that wants to consume it. But even microscopic animals hunt and eat each other.

The daphnia are also very tiny, sometimes as small as only 0.2 millimeters long. These microscopic creatures have heads, five or six pairs of legs, compound eyes, antennae, and even hearts! The daphnia can actually get drunk on alcohol, and under the microscope, scientists have seen their heart rates escalate when under the influence of nicotine or caffeine. It's probably pretty easy for the immortal hydra to hunt down and eat drunk daphnia that are loitering on the edges of the pond algae.

The hydra itself is no single-celled algae. It is also a real animal, with a nervous system and respiration. However, the hydra is pretty dumb, having no brain, and it's not exactly a hunk, having no muscle.

However, brainless as it is, the simple hydra is smart enough to live forever. If a scientist rips the hydra to shreds, in fact, into pieces so small that they are single cells, the animal will regroup and form a whole hydra again! A 1998 study by Associate Professor Daniel E. Martinez of Pomona College wrote, "To test for the presence or absence of aging in hydra, mortality and reproductive rates for three hydra cohorts have been analyzed for a period of four years. The results provide no evidence for aging in hydra: mortality rates have remained extremely low and there are no apparent signs of decline in reproductive rates. Hydra may have indeed escaped senescence and may be potentially immortal."[1]

So if the hydra can live forever, why not the vampire? It would be one thing to argue that we've never witnessed any immortality in animal life, but that is simply not the case.

Immortality could be possible for the vampire in a similar way that it exists for the hydra. This may be why vampire folklore, including the Twilight series, insists that any vampiric remains be totally burned to prohibit any possibility of the vampiric pieces regrouping and reforming the creature. If hydra cells can regroup and recreate the animal, why can't the vampire's cells do the same thing?

Regrowth of lost limbs, commonly thought of as tissue regeneration, is a hot topic among today's scientists. Merely chopping off a vampire's limbs or ripping him to shreds may not suffice to kill him. What if the vampire can regrow his lost limbs or regenerate the tissue that the vampire killer has severed or destroyed? There is a reason why Edward Cullen must not only rip Victoria into pieces but also burn the remains into ashes. It is quite possible that vampires can regenerate themselves, just as people thought in the ancient villages.

Steven Scadding, professor of integrative biology at the University of Guelph in Ontario, Canada, has been studying tissue regeneration for more than twenty-five years, with a primary focus on *axolotls*, a species of salamanders that possess this regenerative power. Scadding has discovered that a substance called retinoic acid, or tretinoin, is one of the main factors in regeneration. An acid form of vitamin A, retinoic acid is very popular

---

1. Daniel E. Martinez, "Mortality Patterns Suggest Lack of Senescence in Hydra," *Experimental Gerontology*, 1998, Vol. 33, No. 3, p. 217.

with older people who are trying to look young. It supposedly helps wrinkles look smoother. Another one of its main uses is fighting acne, so if you want to be an immortal vampire with clear skin, perhaps retinoic acid is the key to your happiness.

More important, retinoic acid supposedly slows the aging of skin. The acid seems to "switch on certain genes, triggering specific growth patterns."[2] Different amounts of acid in the blastema (the skin covering that grows over the stump of the removed limb) regulates how the limb grows back for *axolotls*. Scadding is investigating how the retinoic acid somehow allows various cells to communicate with one another and grow in the proper place.[3]

Scadding hopes to learn how *axolotls* regenerate and apply that knowledge to human beings. "If amphibians can do it, and they have an arrangement of bones, muscles, and cells similar to ours, there should be the potential for humans to do it, too," he says.[4]

Another example, among many others, of researchers working on limb and nerve regeneration is Professor Lyn Beasley, the head of the Department of Zoology at the University of Western Australia, who is leading a team trying to discover how simple animals regrow nerve fibers. Their goal is to discover a cure for damaged nervous systems in human beings.

Some nerves in our body, including those in our fingers and hands, do grow back when cut. Unfortunately, that's not the case with the nerves in our central nervous system. Those nerves try

2. Anne LeBold, "What Stimulates Limb Regeneration?" *Research*, Summer 1995, http://www.uoguelph.ca/research/publications/Assets/HTML_MAGS/oasis/evolution3.html.
3. This section is derived in part from: Lois H. Gresh and Robert Weinberg, *The Science of Supervillains* (New York, NY: John Wiley & Sons, Inc., 2004), pp.71–79.
4. Anne LeBold, "What Stimulates Limb Regeneration?" *Research*, Summer 1995.

to regrow for a few days and then stop. No one is sure why. Dr. Beasley and her team have been studying animals to see if they can learn the secret from them.

Lizards were among the first animals selected for limb regeneration. A lizard can have its optic nerve smashed and the nerve fibers will regrow from the brain to the eye within half a year. However, that growth isn't always perfect. Sometimes, the nerves grow to the wrong section of the brain. The lizard is capable of regrowing nerve cells but not always to the right location. Which prompted Dr. Beasley and her team to look at an even simpler animal than a lizard: a frog.

Frogs regrow nerve fibers to the right place in the brain, but it takes them much longer to perform this feat than it takes lizards. Not satisfied with the time factor, Beasley went searching for another animal that could regrow nerve fibers quickly. After much looking, she discovered goldfish.

Crush the optic nerve of a goldfish, and immediately, hundreds of thousands of optic nerve cells begin rebuilding the path between the severed eye and the brain. In approximately one month, the goldfish's 20–20 vision is completely restored. The small fish possesses the right molecules to duplicate nerve cells and also possesses the chemical guideposts to direct the nerve growth to the proper area of the brain.

While Dr. Beasley and her team haven't yet discovered exactly how these special molecules and chemical guides work, they have plenty of test subjects to study and have high hopes of someday being able to apply what they learn to the human nervous system.

Which leads us with just the slightest stretch of the imagination to the planarian, a quarter-of-an-inch-long worm that can live in the ocean, in lakes, and in the earth without any problem. It's also a popular subject for experiments in sophomore biology classes because when you cut off its head, the planarian has the enviable talent of being able to grow it back.

If the vampire is anything like the planarian, merely cutting off his head isn't going to kill him. You'll have to burn the vampire to totally destroy him.

Some planarians, which are also known as flatworms, reproduce in a unique manner. A planarian stretches until its body pulls apart into two pieces. The section with the head grows a new body, while the section that's all body grows a new head. Interesting stuff, but flatworms and humans are far apart on the evolutionary scale. We're very distant cousins. Yet distance in biology may be closer than most people realize.

According to Dr. Sanchez Alvarado, a researcher at the University of Utah Health Sciences Center, 70 percent of the 4,500 genes that researchers have studied in planarians are found in people.[5] By studying planarians, Alvarado hopes to learn the processes behind regeneration and apply them to human medicine.

Planarians are metazoans. That is, they're animals that originate from a single cell and grow into complex organisms with cells arranged into different organs. They're one of a number of metazoans that regenerate. Salamanders are another.

A tissue sample as small as 1/279th of an inch can be taken from just about any part of a planarian and will regenerate the entire worm. That's comparable to a person losing a finger in an accident, and the finger growing an exact duplicate of the victim.

Scientists suspect the secret of a planarian's regeneration lies

---

5. Phil Sahm, "The Mystery of Regeneration," *Health Sciences Report*, University of Utah Health Sciences Center, Summer 2003, p. 1.

with the vast number of cells called neoblasts contained in its body. Neoblasts can transform into whatever cells a planarian needs. They can become neurons if the planarian needs neurons, or they can become muscle cells if the planarian needs muscle cells. Scientists aren't sure how many neoblasts are required to regrow an entire worm. Dr. Alvarado thinks one neoblast might be enough to do the job. "In principle," says Alvarado, talking about the flatworms, "they are immortal."[6]

If all this sounds vaguely familiar, it's because neoblasts have been in the news during the past few years. In humans, they are usually called stem cells.

Basically, there are methods of antiaging and immortality already available in nature. If a vampire is already dead as a human, it's conceivable that he can stop aging and can even achieve a sense of immortality.

But would it really be all that fun to live forever? If your time on Earth is infinite, wouldn't you lose all desire to do anything? For a procrastinator, who puts everything off until the last minute, having forever to get anything done would mean turning into a thousand-year-old couch potato.

On the other hand, if you like to paint or write, having eternal life could eventually increase your skills to the point where you are a magnificent painter or an extremely accomplished writer. (Clearly, I haven't lived forever, or I'd currently be polishing off my forty-thousand-page series of sixty intertwined novels rather than polishing off this book about Stephenie Meyer's Twilight Saga.)

But even if you do love the arts or have a passion for something special, such as playing the violin, having forever to do

6. Ibid, page 2.

your "thing" is most likely too long a time period. Everything can become tedious and dull after, say, a thousand years. Who wants to write love poems for a thousand years, or more? So you like gardening, but do you really want to pot zinnias for seven hundred years?

I touched on these issues of immortality in the beginning of this book. Living forever with the same person could drive you mad. People, even vampires who were *once* people, change over the course of a normal lifetime. A woman who is crazy in love with her husband may despise and resent him ten years down the road. A man who adores his wife may get tired of the same old jokes and routines. Friends often fall apart after months or years, as do brothers and sisters. People *change*. So being stuck with the same vampire husband for eternity, thousands and thousands, millions and millions of years, could be a very bad thing.

If your vampire man is one in a trillion and the two of you actually get along happily for thousands of years, you're in luck. But what happens if a vampire killer comes along, rips your guy into shreds, and burns the remains into ashes? If indeed you are in the state of only "one man for me" and "my Edward and I are true soul mates," then you have literally eternity to spend all alone now. Without your only soul mate, immortality is going to be so incredibly lonely that you may try to rip yourself into shreds and burn the remains.

CHAPTER 17

MENTAL TELEPATHY AND SEEING THE FUTURE

✧

Like all vampires, the ones in the Twilight Saga possess some amazing powers. In addition to having the strength of Superman, Edward runs so fast that Bella can barely see him, and his endurance is stunning. It seems nothing can tire Edward and the other members of the Cullen family.

However, vampires, including those in the Cullen family, possess traits that are far more amazing than mere superhuman strength and the speed of supersonic jets. They also read minds and project their own thoughts into other people's minds. They sometimes can predict what's going to happen in the future.

Edward can read anybody's mind, except for Bella's mind, as she is somehow immune to his thought probes. In fact, he can read minds that are within a radius of several miles from his location. He can also project his thoughts into Bella's mind and often does so in order to keep her out of danger and give her guidance.

Imagine what it would be like to have the ability to read everyone else's mind within a radius of several miles. You would need a way to turn off all those thoughts, or your brain would become as cluttered with other people's thoughts as the freeways are jammed with cars. There would be way too much traffic coursing through your brain at all times. How would you sort through the thoughts of thousands of people all at once just to listen to a particular person's thoughts? And what if that particular person happened to be two miles away? You would not know that he was there, so it would be impossible to sift through thousands of other people's thoughts to find the person you want to hear. Of course, being like Edward, your sense of smell would be heightened, so you might be able to smell the person you want to hear, then somehow pinpoint his brain and read his mind. This implies that you would need a way to sort through the smells of thousands of people, too, just to identify the smell of the person you want to hear.

Bella is lucky that Edward cannot read her mind. It would be creepy to be with a boyfriend who is constantly reading your every thought. Nothing would be private. He might misinterpret all sorts of stray thoughts that really don't mean anything.

However, as noted, he can project his own thoughts into her mind. When she's in trouble and her life is at risk, he often comes to the rescue simply by telling her what to do and where to go using mental projection. He does not use hypnosis, which is very common in other vampire stories.

Mental telepathy is the subject of many science fiction and fantasy stories, and a lot of people wonder what it would be like to read the minds of those around them. It is one aspect of a much bigger field of study known as parapsychology.

Most parapsychology studies, however, focus on mental telepathy and extrasensory perception. Other types of parapsychology include things like using your mind to move objects or blow things up, which is collectively referred to as "psychokinesis." Some people call the study of these phenomena "psionics."

Jasper Hale has a form of psychic power that differs from Edward's mental telepathy. Jasper can not only feel other people's emotions, he can manipulate their emotions, as well. This is sometimes known as "clairsentience," a form of extrasensory perception that enables someone to clearly sense how other people feel.

Scientists tend to think of mental telepathy and related matters as pseudoscience because no proof exists that these things have ever happened. Repeated scientific studies have failed to demonstrate anyone's ability to read minds.

However, every culture throughout history has reported incidents of psychic phenomena. All over the world, earlier scientists and public leaders believed in mental telepathy and other psychic abilities.

When the scientific revolution began in the first few years of the 1800s, scientists were known as natural philosophers, later, in 1834, to be called scientists. Many of these natural philosophers, including Isaac Newton, believed that alchemy was real, as well as other forms of magic.

So during the time when vampirism was believed to be true by many people, it also made sense to them that the vampires might have extrasensory powers. But it wasn't mental telepathy that was considered a power of vampires. Instead, it was the ability to hypnotize humans and make them do whatever the vampire wanted.

During the period known as the Enlightenment, which came after the scientific revolution, folklore and strict adherence to rules simply dictated by tradition started to diminish more rapidly. This isn't to say that folklore and tradition disappeared, not by any stretch of the imagination, but rather, that many people started viewing things in more rational and logical ways. For example, so-called enlightened people saw the universe as a mechanistic, deterministic system, which means the world around us could be explored, studied, and analyzed until we could figure out how it worked. Calculations and reasoning became more important than myth and folktales. Enlightened people thought that psychic wonders were pure fantasy and totally irrational.

Enlightened people back then probably would not believe in vampires, for example. They might believe that corpses became bloated and that people died from as-yet-unknown causes, but without proof, they may not have admitted believing in the walking dead.

Hypnosis was once known as *mesmerism*, a term coined in honor of Franz Anton Mesmer, who was born in 1734 and died in 1815. He was a Viennese physician and believer in Enlightenment values.

During Mesmer's lifetime, scientists did not know what electricity and magnetism really were, and both were considered to be invisible fluids of some kind. Then along came Franz Mesmer, who believed he had found yet another invisible fluid, which he termed *animal magnetism*.

Mesmer's animal magnetism had nothing to do with the realms of the supernatural, such as vampires, mental telepathy, and psychic powers. But he did think that his animal magnetism could heal the sick and help people do things they wouldn't ordinarily do. I've given you a couple of clues as to what animal magnetism was, so can you guess by now?

Clue #1. Hypnosis was once known as mesmerism.

Clue #2. Animal magnetism could heal the sick and help people do things they wouldn't ordinarily do.

Clue #3. Animal magnetism had nothing to do with the realms of the supernatural, such as vampires, mental telepathy, and psychic powers.

In short, animal magnetism was another way of saying mesmerism. And of course, mesmerism was hypnosis.

Franz Mesmer, a physician and enlightened scientist, developed the methods of hypnosis still used by many practicers of the idea today. And more interesting, he believed that under hypnosis, people had the ability to be clairvoyants, or psychics.

Keep in mind that psychics supposedly can hypnotize others, read minds, project their thoughts into other people's minds, and see the future. These are all attributes given to the vampires in the Twilight Saga.

As famous as Franz Mesmer and his hypnotism became, it didn't take long for other scientists to reject his claims. In 1784, the French Royal Society of Medicine and the French Academy of Sciences both did extensive studies of mesmerism. Both studies concluded that there was no evidence that mesmerism worked, much less psychic phenomena.

Belief in mesmerism faded by the 1850s, but the emerging spiritualist movement helped revitalize the idea. People claiming to be hypnotized supposedly did incredible things while they were in trances. Spiritual mediums rose in popularity throughout Europe, and many people hired mediums to help them contact their dead family members and friends.

DANIEL DUNGLAS HOME, FAMOUS SPIRITUAL MEDIUM

Daniel Dunglas Home was one of the most infamous spiritual mediums in the entire nineteenth century. Born in 1833 in Edinburgh, Scotland, Daniel Dunglas Home moved to America in 1842. When he was a teenager, Home claimed that he could

(continued)

move furniture simply by using his mind. He would want a chair to move from the living room to the kitchen, and the chair would do as he commanded.

In today's world, a teenager like Home would be put in a "home" for the mentally ill. And in fact, Home was thrown out of school for "demonstrating poltergeist activity" to other students.

But back then, a lot of people were still more open to the unusual and strange. Home's minister encouraged him to exercise his ability to move objects using his mind. He also encouraged him to use his gift to help others in the community.

Home started holding séances.

During his séances, attended by many people, furniture rose into the air, an accordion locked in a cabinet played without any human intervention, and loud knocking sounds were heard that made no sense beyond the notion that spirits were causing them.

Then in 1852, at the age of twenty-one, Home levitated during one of his séances. Not only could he lift furniture by commanding it to rise using his mind, but now he could actually lift himself into the air simply by wishing it so.

At this point, Daniel Dunglas Home became quite famous as a spiritual medium. Three years later, he toured extensively throughout Europe and Russia, demonstrating his psychic abilities.

Of course, there were plenty of people who claimed that Home was a fraud. But nobody could ever explain how he lifted and moved furniture, played accordions that were locked in cabinets, or lifted himself high into the air. Because nobody could figure out how he performed supposed stage illusions, to many, his psychic abilities seemed real.

While science flourished in the nineteenth century, highly religious people clung to their beliefs. The supernatural had to be real; mental telepathy, hypnotism, vampires: why shouldn't they exist if indeed God, Satan, and all the angels existed?

But then science actually merged for a while with the supernatural. In 1882, the Society for Psychical Research, or SPR, was founded in London. It was so successful that by 1887, its council included eight members of the British Royal Society. The SPR published a yearly report about its psychic research, and it was so popular that an American SPR was created, as well as other psychic societies across Europe.

Most of the SPR research tried to test the abilities of spiritual mediums and other people who thought they possessed psychic abilities. Cards and dice were used, as well, and overall, the scientific community did not particularly trust the results of the SPR experiments.

In 1927, J. B. Rhine and others at Duke University used ESP cards developed by Karl Zener to perform a series of psychic experiments. Rhine's techniques were much more sophisticated and controlled than those used by the SPR. He used statistics to measure results and included ordinary people in his experiments. His 1934 book *Extra Sensory Perception* put the term ESP into everyday language. His 1937 book *New Frontiers of the Mind* was extremely influential, and together, both books made the study of mental telepathy and other forms of ESP respectable. Duke University created the first serious and long-term university-established laboratory for parapsychology experiments. The laboratory later became known as the Rhine Research Center. In addition, the *Journal of Parapsychology*, which is still published today, was established by Rhine and others in 1937.

During the 1970s and 1980s, the United States government

authorized and paid for several ESP investigations. Project Stargate, for example, used the ESP talent called "remote viewing," whereby the medium can see what is happening as far away as hundreds of miles. But to date, none of these projects has yielded proof of ESP powers.

For those of you who believe in paranormal powers such as mental telepathy, and those of you who hope that people (and vampires) can have these powers, a few studies have been done that conclude that the powers exist. For example, at the University of California—Davis, statistics professor Jessica Utts performs studies of psychic powers. She teaches college classes such as Integrated Studies: Testing Psychic Claims. If you look at her faculty Web site,[1] you'll see a list of parapsychology research papers and labs.

As for seeing the future, Alice Cullen has the power, but it does have its limitations. She knows the end results of what will happen, but she does not always know how or why things will happen. When werewolves are involved, Alice's ability to see the future diminishes and becomes muddled.

For thousands of years, people all over the world have believed in psychic powers and the ability to foresee the future. One early story about seeing the future was from *The Iliad* and *The Odyssey*. In that story, Apollo placed a curse on Cassandra, so that she could see what was going to happen, but nobody ever believed her. She knew, for example, that the Greeks would conquer the city of Troy, but her father Priam, the King of Troy, refused to heed her warnings.

Much later, in the late 1800s and early 1900s, many novels featured women in danger who escaped death because of psychic

---

1. http://anson.ucdavis.edu/~utts.

powers. Thrillers often featured lost races and tribes with psy-chic powers; some examples are *She* by H. Rider Haggard (1887), *Thyra—of the Polar Pit* by Robert Ames Bennett (1900), and *Eric of the Strong Heart* by Victor Rousseau (1914). In 1930, Olaf Sta-pledon's *The Last and First Men* suggested that over the next sev-eral billion years, humans would evolve to have enormous psychic powers. Stories about mental telepathy and seeing the future were prominent in the science fiction magazines of the 1930s and 1940s.

So the ideas that Edward can read minds and Alice can see the future are not new ideas. However, it's a creative and interesting twist that Edward can read anyone's mind except for Bella Swan's.

CHAPTER 18

ROMANCE QUIZ:

Could Edward Be the Man for You?

✧

Almost every girl who reads the Twilight Saga wishes that a guy just like Edward would walk into her biology class. But are you and Edward (or someone like him) really compatible? This chapter helps you find out whether the Edward in your life is really your true one and only love.

First, I assume that you are a female. (If not, just pretend for the purposes of this test that you are a girl.) I also assume that you are a teenager, but just to be safe, write your age here: _____

Next, be very honest and describe yourself based on the listed statements and the ranks you give to them. For example, if the first statement is "I am an idiot" and you know that you are smart, then you would answer, "Not at all characteristic of me." On the other hand, if you get lots of C's in class and learning is extremely difficult for you, you might answer, "Moderately characteristic of me." If an attribute is listed as "Sweet and caring," and you wish that you were sweet and caring but you know that deep inside, you really don't care about anyone but yourself (and you also beat your dog and set your cat's tail on fire whenever you get the chance), then you should answer, "Not at all characteristic of me" (and if you beat your dog and set your cat's tail on fire, you should also get therapy right away). On the other hand, if you are sometimes sweet and caring, but you often act in unkind ways that hurt people (even though you don't intend to hurt them), then you might answer, "Moderately characteristic of me."

Now get your pencils sharpened, and here we go!

Statement #1. I am sweet and caring.
___ Not at all characteristic of me
___ Sometimes characteristic of me
___ Moderately characteristic of me
___ Very characteristic of me
___ Extremely characteristic of me

Statement #2. I am critical of other people, and I often leap to conclusions about them that are not necessarily accurate or just.
___ Not at all characteristic of me
___ Sometimes characteristic of me
___ Moderately characteristic of me
___ Very characteristic of me
___ Extremely characteristic of me

Statement #3. I am a patient person.
___ Not at all characteristic of me
___ Sometimes characteristic of me
___ Moderately characteristic of me
___ Very characteristic of me
___ Extremely characteristic of me

Statement #4. When I disagree with someone, I keep my mouth shut until I've had enough time to think about my response.
___ Not at all characteristic of me

___ Sometimes characteristic of me
___ Moderately characteristic of me
___ Very characteristic of me
___ Extremely characteristic of me

Statement #5. I probably whine and complain too much. I don't mean to be this way, and sometimes, people think that I'm complaining when I'm just pointing out how to make things better.
___ Not at all characteristic of me
___ Sometimes characteristic of me
___ Moderately characteristic of me
___ Very characteristic of me
___ Extremely characteristic of me

Statement #6. Sometimes I'm really happy, but sometimes my mood drops and I get extremely depressed.
___ Not at all characteristic of me
___ Sometimes characteristic of me
___ Moderately characteristic of me
___ Very characteristic of me
___ Extremely characteristic of me

Statement #7. I always tell people exactly what I think of them.
___ Not at all characteristic of me
___ Sometimes characteristic of me
___ Moderately characteristic of me
___ Very characteristic of me
___ Extremely characteristic of me

Statement #8. I believe that everyone has the right to be themselves, to be unique, to act differently from other people, and to think what they want. I know that my friends have faults, but I tend to be very accepting of them anyway, and when my friends whine and complain too much, I tend to overlook their behavior. Sometimes, I think that I am too tolerant of other people's faults.

___ Not at all characteristic of me
___ Sometimes characteristic of me
___ Moderately characteristic of me
___ Very characteristic of me
___ Extremely characteristic of me

Statement #9. More often than not, it's tough for me even to know what to say to people.

___ Not at all characteristic of me
___ Sometimes characteristic of me
___ Moderately characteristic of me
___ Very characteristic of me
___ Extremely characteristic of me

Statement #10. I crack a lot of jokes, and usually when people are with me, they laugh a lot and have a good time.

___ Not at all characteristic of me
___ Sometimes characteristic of me
___ Moderately characteristic of me
___ Very characteristic of me
___ Extremely characteristic of me

Statement #11. My friends usually do what I want to do. I tend to dominate other people and get my way. I am something of a control freak.

___ Not at all characteristic of me

___ Sometimes characteristic of me
___ Moderately characteristic of me
___ Very characteristic of me
___ Extremely characteristic of me

Statement #12. I am a loving person.
___ Not at all characteristic of me
___ Sometimes characteristic of me
___ Moderately characteristic of me
___ Very characteristic of me
___ Extremely characteristic of me

Statement #13. I have no problem saying exactly what's on my mind—almost all the time.
___ Not at all characteristic of me
___ Sometimes characteristic of me
___ Moderately characteristic of me
___ Very characteristic of me
___ Extremely characteristic of me

Statement #14. I am athletic and try to keep in shape.
___ Not at all characteristic of me
___ Sometimes characteristic of me
___ Moderately characteristic of me
___ Very characteristic of me
___ Extremely characteristic of me

Statement #15. When I have something to say, I speak up right away. I don't hesitate before talking.
___ Not at all characteristic of me
___ Sometimes characteristic of me

___ Moderately characteristic of me
___ Very characteristic of me
___ Extremely characteristic of me

Statement #16. I have a really hard time getting people to understand what I'm trying to tell them. It's hard for me to express myself.
___ Not at all characteristic of me
___ Sometimes characteristic of me
___ Moderately characteristic of me
___ Very characteristic of me
___ Extremely characteristic of me

Statement #17. When things get emotional and people disagree, I have a hard time arguing for my opinion.
___ Not at all characteristic of me
___ Sometimes characteristic of me
___ Moderately characteristic of me
___ Very characteristic of me
___ Extremely characteristic of me

Statement #18. I do what I want when I want to do it.
___ Not at all characteristic of me
___ Sometimes characteristic of me
___ Moderately characteristic of me
___ Very characteristic of me
___ Extremely characteristic of me

Statement #19. Nobody can tell me what to do.
___ Not at all characteristic of me
___ Sometimes characteristic of me

___ Moderately characteristic of me

___ Very characteristic of me

___ Extremely characteristic of me

Statement #20. I go along with what other people want to do. It usually doesn't matter to me very much at all.

___ Not at all characteristic of me

___ Sometimes characteristic of me

___ Moderately characteristic of me

___ Very characteristic of me

___ Extremely characteristic of me

Statement #21. I am an angry person.

___ Not at all characteristic of me

___ Sometimes characteristic of me

___ Moderately characteristic of me

___ Very characteristic of me

___ Extremely characteristic of me

Statement #22. I am a tolerant person.

___ Not at all characteristic of me

___ Sometimes characteristic of me

___ Moderately characteristic of me

___ Very characteristic of me

___ Extremely characteristic of me

Statement #23. I am an intelligent person.

___ Not at all characteristic of me

___ Sometimes characteristic of me

___ Moderately characteristic of me

___ Very characteristic of me
___ Extremely characteristic of me

Statement #24. I am a creative person.
___ Not at all characteristic of me
___ Sometimes characteristic of me
___ Moderately characteristic of me
___ Very characteristic of me
___ Extremely characteristic of me

Statement #25. I am a physically beautiful person.
___ Not at all characteristic of me
___ Sometimes characteristic of me
___ Moderately characteristic of me
___ Very characteristic of me
___ Extremely characteristic of me

Statement #26. I am a lazy person.
___ Not at all characteristic of me
___ Sometimes characteristic of me
___ Moderately characteristic of me
___ Very characteristic of me
___ Extremely characteristic of me

Statement #27. I work hard.
___ Not at all characteristic of me
___ Sometimes characteristic of me
___ Moderately characteristic of me
___ Very characteristic of me
___ Extremely characteristic of me

Statement #28. I am a highly emotional person.

___ Not at all characteristic of me

___ Sometimes characteristic of me

___ Moderately characteristic of me

___ Very characteristic of me

___ Extremely characteristic of me

Statement #29. I am a submissive person.

___ Not at all characteristic of me

___ Sometimes characteristic of me

___ Moderately characteristic of me

___ Very characteristic of me

___ Extremely characteristic of me

Statement #30. I am a friendly person.

___ Not at all characteristic of me

___ Sometimes characteristic of me

___ Moderately characteristic of me

___ Very characteristic of me

___ Extremely characteristic of me

Statement #31. Most of my friends are restless and upset a lot.

___ Not at all characteristic of me

___ Sometimes characteristic of me

___ Moderately characteristic of me

___ Very characteristic of me

___ Extremely characteristic of me

Statement #32. Most of my friends are tolerant people.

___ Not at all characteristic of me

___ Sometimes characteristic of me

___ Moderately characteristic of me
___ Very characteristic of me
___ Extremely characteristic of me

Statement #33. Most of my friends are intelligent people.
___ Not at all characteristic of me
___ Sometimes characteristic of me
___ Moderately characteristic of me
___ Very characteristic of me
___ Extremely characteristic of me

Statement #34. Most of my friends are creative people.
___ Not at all characteristic of me
___ Sometimes characteristic of me
___ Moderately characteristic of me
___ Very characteristic of me
___ Extremely characteristic of me

Statement #35. Most of my friends are physically beautiful people.
___ Not at all characteristic of me
___ Sometimes characteristic of me
___ Moderately characteristic of me
___ Very characteristic of me
___ Extremely characteristic of me

Statement #36. Most of my friends are boring people.
___ Not at all characteristic of me
___ Sometimes characteristic of me
___ Moderately characteristic of me
___ Very characteristic of me
___ Extremely characteristic of me

Statement #37. Most of my friends work hard.

___ Not at all characteristic of me

___ Sometimes characteristic of me

___ Moderately characteristic of me

___ Very characteristic of me

___ Extremely characteristic of me

Statement #38. Most of my friends are highly emotional people.

___ Not at all characteristic of me

___ Sometimes characteristic of me

___ Moderately characteristic of me

___ Very characteristic of me

___ Extremely characteristic of me

Statement #39. Most of my friends are submissive people.

___ Not at all characteristic of me

___ Sometimes characteristic of me

___ Moderately characteristic of me

___ Very characteristic of me

___ Extremely characteristic of me

Statement #40. Most of my friends are outgoing, sociable people.

___ Not at all characteristic of me

___ Sometimes characteristic of me

___ Moderately characteristic of me

___ Very characteristic of me

___ Extremely characteristic of me

Statement #41. If someone compliments a friend of mine, I feel as happy as if I had received the compliment.

___ Not at all characteristic of me

___ Sometimes characteristic of me
___ Moderately characteristic of me
___ Very characteristic of me
___ Extremely characteristic of me

Statement #42. If someone compliments a friend of mine, I get jealous.
___ Not at all characteristic of me
___ Sometimes characteristic of me
___ Moderately characteristic of me
___ Very characteristic of me
___ Extremely characteristic of me

Statement #43. If someone insults a friend of mine, it's as if he has insulted me, as well.
___ Not at all characteristic of me
___ Sometimes characteristic of me
___ Moderately characteristic of me
___ Very characteristic of me
___ Extremely characteristic of me

Statement #44. If someone insults a friend of mine, I will stand up and defend my friend.
___ Not at all characteristic of me
___ Sometimes characteristic of me
___ Moderately characteristic of me
___ Very characteristic of me
___ Extremely characteristic of me

Statement #45. If someone insults a friend of mine, I keep my distance from the friend until things settle down.

___ Not at all characteristic of me

___ Sometimes characteristic of me

___ Moderately characteristic of me

___ Very characteristic of me

___ Extremely characteristic of me

Statement #46. It matters a lot to me what other people think about my friends.

___ Not at all characteristic of me

___ Sometimes characteristic of me

___ Moderately characteristic of me

___ Very characteristic of me

___ Extremely characteristic of me

Statement #47. I would sacrifice my life to save a friend or family member.

___ Not at all characteristic of me

___ Sometimes characteristic of me

___ Moderately characteristic of me

___ Very characteristic of me

___ Extremely characteristic of me

Statement #48. I would sacrifice my life to save a family member but not a friend.

___ Not at all characteristic of me

___ Sometimes characteristic of me

___ Moderately characteristic of me

___ Very characteristic of me

___ Extremely characteristic of me

Statement #49. I would sacrifice my life if someone offered my family and friends a million dollars.

___ Not at all characteristic of me

___ Sometimes characteristic of me

___ Moderately characteristic of me

___ Very characteristic of me

___ Extremely characteristic of me

Statement #50. I believe in revenge: an eye for an eye, a tooth for a tooth.

___ Not at all characteristic of me

___ Sometimes characteristic of me

___ Moderately characteristic of me

___ Very characteristic of me

___ Extremely characteristic of me

Statement #51. If someone was beating up or otherwise assaulting a friend of mine, I would step in and try to fight him off, even if I'm not very strong.

___ Not at all characteristic of me

___ Sometimes characteristic of me

___ Moderately characteristic of me

___ Very characteristic of me

___ Extremely characteristic of me

Statement #52. I respect people who spend their lives helping other people. I would like to help people as much as possible, too.

___ Not at all characteristic of me

___ Sometimes characteristic of me

___ Moderately characteristic of me

___ Very characteristic of me
___ Extremely characteristic of me

Statement #53. If I could do something to save the world's animals from being hunted or hurt in some way, I would do it. I believe that animals suffer and have feelings, too.
___ Not at all characteristic of me
___ Sometimes characteristic of me
___ Moderately characteristic of me
___ Very characteristic of me
___ Extremely characteristic of me

Statement #54. I think that all babies are cute.
___ Not at all characteristic of me
___ Sometimes characteristic of me
___ Moderately characteristic of me
___ Very characteristic of me
___ Extremely characteristic of me

Statement #55. If someone gives me a gift that I don't particularly like or that I think isn't cool enough, I will make fun of the gift in front of the person.
___ Not at all characteristic of me
___ Sometimes characteristic of me
___ Moderately characteristic of me
___ Very characteristic of me
___ Extremely characteristic of me

SCORING

For each statement, I give you a range of points to add to your total score depending on your answer. For example, here are the scores for Statement #1:

Statement #1. I am sweet and caring.

 _0_ Not at all characteristic of me

 _0_ Sometimes characteristic of me

 _2_ Moderately characteristic of me

 _4_ Very characteristic of me

 _5_ Extremely characteristic of me

So if you answered "Extremely characteristic of me," give yourself 5 points. If you answered "Moderately characteristic of me," give yourself 2 points. If you answered "Very characteristic of me," give yourself 4 points. You get the idea!

After you add all of your points together for every statement, I'll tell you if you're compatible with a guy like Edward. *You will find out if a guy like Edward is going to have the hots for you.* If so, then next time you're in biology class, start looking around for Mr. Perfect because he might be sitting there, right next to you!

Now, you already have your score for Statement #1, so we'll skip that one and move forward with Statement #2.

Statement #2. I am critical of other people, and I often leap to conclusions about them that are not necessarily accurate or just.

 _5_ Not at all characteristic of me

 _4_ Sometimes characteristic of me

 _4_ Moderately characteristic of me

 _2_ Very characteristic of me

 _0_ Extremely characteristic of me

Statement #3. I am a patient person.

 _0_ Not at all characteristic of me

 _2_ Sometimes characteristic of me

 _4_ Moderately characteristic of me

  _4_ Very characteristic of me
  _5_ Extremely characteristic of me

Statement #4. When I disagree with someone, I keep my mouth shut until I've had enough time to think about my response.
  _5_ Not at all characteristic of me
  _5_ Sometimes characteristic of me
  _5_ Moderately characteristic of me
  _3_ Very characteristic of me
  _3_ Extremely characteristic of me

Statement #5. I probably whine and complain too much. I don't mean to be this way, and sometimes, people think that I'm complaining when I'm just pointing out how to make things better.
  _5_ Not at all characteristic of me
  _4_ Sometimes characteristic of me
  _2_ Moderately characteristic of me
  _0_ Very characteristic of me
  _0_ Extremely characteristic of me

Statement #6. Sometimes I'm really happy, but sometimes my mood drops and I get extremely depressed.
  _5_ Not at all characteristic of me
  _4_ Sometimes characteristic of me
  _2_ Moderately characteristic of me
  _1_ Very characteristic of me
  _0_ Extremely characteristic of me

Statement #7. I always tell people exactly what I think of them.
  _3_ Not at all characteristic of me
  _4_ Sometimes characteristic of me

  _5_ Moderately characteristic of me
  _1_ Very characteristic of me
  _0_ Extremely characteristic of me

Statement #8. I believe that everyone has the right to be themselves, to be unique, to act differently from other people, and to think what they want. I know that my friends have faults, but I tend to be very accepting of them anyway, and when my friends whine and complain too much, I tend to overlook their behavior. Sometimes, I think that I am too tolerant of other people's faults.

  _0_ Not at all characteristic of me
  _1_ Sometimes characteristic of me
  _3_ Moderately characteristic of me
  _5_ Very characteristic of me
  _5_ Extremely characteristic of me

Statement #9. More often than not, it's tough for me even to know what to say to people.

  _5_ Not at all characteristic of me
  _4_ Sometimes characteristic of me
  _2_ Moderately characteristic of me
  _0_ Very characteristic of me
  _0_ Extremely characteristic of me

Statement #10. I crack a lot of jokes, and usually when people are with me, they laugh a lot and have a good time.

  _0_ Not at all characteristic of me
  _5_ Sometimes characteristic of me
  _5_ Moderately characteristic of me
  _5_ Very characteristic of me
  _5_ Extremely characteristic of me

Statement #11. My friends usually do what I want to do. I tend to dominate other people and get my way. I am something of a control freak.

  _3_ Not at all characteristic of me
  _5_ Sometimes characteristic of me
  _5_ Moderately characteristic of me
  _3_ Very characteristic of me
  _0_ Extremely characteristic of me

Statement #12. I am a loving person.

  _0_ Not at all characteristic of me
  _0_ Sometimes characteristic of me
  _0_ Moderately characteristic of me
  _5_ Very characteristic of me
  _5_ Extremely characteristic of me

Statement #13. I have no problem saying exactly what's on my mind—almost all the time.

  _0_ Not at all characteristic of me
  _5_ Sometimes characteristic of me
  _5_ Moderately characteristic of me
  _5_ Very characteristic of me
  _5_ Extremely characteristic of me

Statement #14. I am athletic and try to keep in shape.

  _0_ Not at all characteristic of me
  _3_ Sometimes characteristic of me
  _3_ Moderately characteristic of me
  _5_ Very characteristic of me
  _5_ Extremely characteristic of me

Statement #15. When I have something to say, I speak up right away. I don't hesitate before talking.

 _0_ Not at all characteristic of me
 _5_ Sometimes characteristic of me
 _5_ Moderately characteristic of me
 _5_ Very characteristic of me
 _5_ Extremely characteristic of me

Statement #16. I have a really hard time getting people to understand what I'm trying to tell them. It's hard for me to express myself.

 _5_ Not at all characteristic of me
 _4_ Sometimes characteristic of me
 _2_ Moderately characteristic of me
 _0_ Very characteristic of me
 _0_ Extremely characteristic of me

Statement #17. When things get emotional and people disagree, I have a hard time arguing for my opinion.

 _0_ Not at all characteristic of me
 _4_ Sometimes characteristic of me
 _5_ Moderately characteristic of me
 _5_ Very characteristic of me
 _0_ Extremely characteristic of me

Statement #18. I do what I want when I want to do it.

 _0_ Not at all characteristic of me
 _5_ Sometimes characteristic of me
 _5_ Moderately characteristic of me
 _3_ Very characteristic of me
 _0_ Extremely characteristic of me

Statement #19. Nobody can tell me what to do.
_5_ Not at all characteristic of me
_5_ Sometimes characteristic of me
_5_ Moderately characteristic of me
_0_ Very characteristic of me
_0_ Extremely characteristic of me

Statement #20. I go along with what other people want to do. It usually doesn't matter to me very much at all.
_0_ Not at all characteristic of me
_3_ Sometimes characteristic of me
_5_ Moderately characteristic of me
_3_ Very characteristic of me
_3_ Extremely characteristic of me

Statement #21. I am an angry person.
_5_ Not at all characteristic of me
_3_ Sometimes characteristic of me
_0_ Moderately characteristic of me
_0_ Very characteristic of me
_0_ Extremely characteristic of me

Statement #22. I am a tolerant person.
_0_ Not at all characteristic of me
_0_ Sometimes characteristic of me
_3_ Moderately characteristic of me
_5_ Very characteristic of me
_5_ Extremely characteristic of me

Statement #23. I am an intelligent person.
_0_ Not at all characteristic of me

 1 Sometimes characteristic of me
 5 Moderately characteristic of me
 5 Very characteristic of me
 5 Extremely characteristic of me

Statement #24. I am a creative person.
 0 Not at all characteristic of me
 5 Sometimes characteristic of me
 5 Moderately characteristic of me
 5 Very characteristic of me
 5 Extremely characteristic of me

Statement #25. I am a physically beautiful person.
 2 Not at all characteristic of me
 4 Sometimes characteristic of me
 5 Moderately characteristic of me
 5 Very characteristic of me
 5 Extremely characteristic of me

Statement #26. I am a lazy person.
 5 Not at all characteristic of me
 2 Sometimes characteristic of me
 2 Moderately characteristic of me
 0 Very characteristic of me
 0 Extremely characteristic of me

Statement #27. I work hard.
 0 Not at all characteristic of me
 3 Sometimes characteristic of me
 4 Moderately characteristic of me
 5 Very characteristic of me
 5 Extremely characteristic of me

Statement #28. I am a highly emotional person.

  _0_ Not at all characteristic of me

  _3_ Sometimes characteristic of me

  _4_ Moderately characteristic of me

  _3_ Very characteristic of me

  _0_ Extremely characteristic of me

Statement #29. I am a submissive person.

  _5_ Not at all characteristic of me

  _5_ Sometimes characteristic of me

  _5_ Moderately characteristic of me

  _0_ Very characteristic of me

  _0_ Extremely characteristic of me

Statement #30. I am a friendly person.

  _0_ Not at all characteristic of me

  _3_ Sometimes characteristic of me

  _3_ Moderately characteristic of me

  _3_ Very characteristic of me

  _3_ Extremely characteristic of me

Statement #31. Most of my friends are restless and upset a lot.

  _0_ Not at all characteristic of me

  _2_ Sometimes characteristic of me

  _4_ Moderately characteristic of me

  _5_ Very characteristic of me

  _5_ Extremely characteristic of me

Statement #32. Most of my friends are tolerant people.

  _0_ Not at all characteristic of me

  _0_ Sometimes characteristic of me

_3_ Moderately characteristic of me

_5_ Very characteristic of me

_5_ Extremely characteristic of me

Statement #33. Most of my friends are intelligent people.

_0_ Not at all characteristic of me

_1_ Sometimes characteristic of me

_5_ Moderately characteristic of me

_5_ Very characteristic of me

_5_ Extremely characteristic of me

Statement #34. Most of my friends are creative people.

_0_ Not at all characteristic of me

_5_ Sometimes characteristic of me

_5_ Moderately characteristic of me

_5_ Very characteristic of me

_5_ Extremely characteristic of me

Statement #35. Most of my friends are physically beautiful people.

_0_ Not at all characteristic of me

_3_ Sometimes characteristic of me

_3_ Moderately characteristic of me

_3_ Very characteristic of me

_3_ Extremely characteristic of me

Statement #36. Most of my friends are boring people.

_5_ Not at all characteristic of me

_4_ Sometimes characteristic of me

_0_ Moderately characteristic of me

_0_ Very characteristic of me

_0_ Extremely characteristic of me

Statement #37. Most of my friends work hard.

  0 Not at all characteristic of me

  3 Sometimes characteristic of me

  3 Moderately characteristic of me

  3 Very characteristic of me

  3 Extremely characteristic of me

Statement #38. Most of my friends are highly emotional people.

  0 Not at all characteristic of me

  3 Sometimes characteristic of me

  3 Moderately characteristic of me

  3 Very characteristic of me

  0 Extremely characteristic of me

Statement #39. Most of my friends are submissive people.

  4 Not at all characteristic of me

  4 Sometimes characteristic of me

  4 Moderately characteristic of me

  0 Very characteristic of me

  0 Extremely characteristic of me

Statement #40. Most of my friends are outgoing, sociable people.

  1 Not at all characteristic of me

  3 Sometimes characteristic of me

  3 Moderately characteristic of me

  3 Very characteristic of me

  3 Extremely characteristic of me

Statement #41. If someone compliments a friend of mine, I feel as happy as if I had received the compliment.

  0 Not at all characteristic of me

__4__ Sometimes characteristic of me
__4__ Moderately characteristic of me
__5__ Very characteristic of me
__5__ Extremely characteristic of me

Statement #42. If someone compliments a friend of mine, I get jealous.
__5__ Not at all characteristic of me
__3__ Sometimes characteristic of me
__0__ Moderately characteristic of me
__0__ Very characteristic of me
__0__ Extremely characteristic of me

Statement #43. If someone insults a friend of mine, it's as if he has insulted me, as well.
__0__ Not at all characteristic of me
__3__ Sometimes characteristic of me
__3__ Moderately characteristic of me
__5__ Very characteristic of me
__5__ Extremely characteristic of me

Statement #44. If someone insults a friend of mine, I will stand up and defend my friend.
__0__ Not at all characteristic of me
__1__ Sometimes characteristic of me
__2__ Moderately characteristic of me
__5__ Very characteristic of me
__5__ Extremely characteristic of me

Statement #45. If someone insults a friend of mine, I keep my distance from the friend until things settle down.

_5_ Not at all characteristic of me

_0_ Sometimes characteristic of me

_0_ Moderately characteristic of me

_0_ Very characteristic of me

_0_ Extremely characteristic of me

Statement #46. It matters a lot to me what other people think about my friends.

_3_ Not at all characteristic of me

_3_ Sometimes characteristic of me

_3_ Moderately characteristic of me

_0_ Very characteristic of me

_0_ Extremely characteristic of me

Statement #47. I would sacrifice my life to save a friend or family member.

_0_ Not at all characteristic of me

_1_ Sometimes characteristic of me

_2_ Moderately characteristic of me

_4_ Very characteristic of me

_5_ Extremely characteristic of me

Statement #48. I would sacrifice my life to save a family member but not a friend.

_0_ Not at all characteristic of me

_1_ Sometimes characteristic of me

_2_ Moderately characteristic of me

_4_ Very characteristic of me

_5_ Extremely characteristic of me

Statement #49. I would sacrifice my life if someone offered my family and friends a million dollars.

 _5_ Not at all characteristic of me
 _0_ Sometimes characteristic of me
 _0_ Moderately characteristic of me
 _0_ Very characteristic of me
 _0_ Extremely characteristic of me

Statement #50. I believe in revenge: an eye for an eye, a tooth for a tooth.

 _0_ Not at all characteristic of me
 _4_ Sometimes characteristic of me
 _0_ Moderately characteristic of me
 _0_ Very characteristic of me
 _0_ Extremely characteristic of me

Statement #51. If someone was beating up or otherwise assaulting a friend of mine, I would step in and try to fight him off, even if I'm not very strong.

 _0_ Not at all characteristic of me
 _1_ Sometimes characteristic of me
 _1_ Moderately characteristic of me
 _5_ Very characteristic of me
 _5_ Extremely characteristic of me

Statement #52. I respect people who spend their lives helping other people. I would like to help people as much as possible, too.

 _0_ Not at all characteristic of me
 _0_ Sometimes characteristic of me
 _2_ Moderately characteristic of me
 _5_ Very characteristic of me
 _5_ Extremely characteristic of me

Statement #53. If I could do something to save the world's animals from being hunted or hurt in some way, I would do it. I believe that animals suffer and have feelings, too.

 _0_ Not at all characteristic of me
 _0_ Sometimes characteristic of me
 _2_ Moderately characteristic of me
 _5_ Very characteristic of me
 _5_ Extremely characteristic of me

Statement #54. I think that all babies are cute.

 _0_ Not at all characteristic of me
 _3_ Sometimes characteristic of me
 _3_ Moderately characteristic of me
 _3_ Very characteristic of me
 _3_ Extremely characteristic of me

Statement #55. If someone gives me a gift that I don't particularly like or that I think isn't cool enough, I will make fun of the gift in front of the person.

 _5_ Not at all characteristic of me
 _3_ Sometimes characteristic of me
 _0_ Moderately characteristic of me
 _0_ Very characteristic of me
 _0_ Extremely characteristic of me

Obviously, a guy like Edward loves a girl like Bella, so for you to have a chance with your Edward kind of guy, you have to possess some of Bella's best qualities. You don't have to be just like Bella—that's probably not possible anyway—but you should be sensitive, caring, and a quick thinker.

With all that in mind, now you can find out if you are indeed compatible with Edward Cullen or someone very similar to him. Check your total score against the following chart.

Total Score	Are you compatible with a guy like Edward?	Additional Comments
< 80	Absolutely not. Give up all hope.	You might want to consider getting psychotherapy.
80–125	There is a slight chance that you will be compatible with a guy like Edward.	You might want to reconsider how sensitive you are to other people, and then take the quiz again. If you score better the second time, you might have a chance to be with a guy like Edward.
126–200	There is a strong possibility that you will be compatible with someone like Edward. However, your perfect guy may not be as perfect as Edward.	If your score is in the range of 150–200, you have a strong chance of finding your own Edward. If your score is lower, in the range of 126–149, your chances are not nearly as strong.
> 200	You win! You are definitely the girl for a handsome, wonderful, perfect vampire guy like Edward! You possess many of Bella Swan's finest qualities, and some of your own, as well.	If your score was more than 230, you are *perfect* for someone like Edward. Now start paying more attention in biology class because he might already be there with you!

HOW THE SCORES WERE TALLIED

In case you're wondering how the scores were tallied, here are the details:

Your Age. First, there is the issue of your age. If you are a teenager, give yourself 50 points. If you are from six to twelve years old, then why do you want to date seventeen-year-old Edward? Shouldn't you find a gorgeous vampire guy who is a little younger? Still, maybe you're wishing to be with someone like Edward when you do become a teenager, so if you're from six to twelve years old, go ahead and give yourself 45 points. You already have good taste in men.

Now, if you're between four and five years old, then I'm wondering why you're reading the Twilight Saga. Shouldn't you be reading Beginning Readers? Still, if you can read books this long and understand them at age four or five, you are so amazing that you deserve 45 points just for being a genius.

However, if you happen to be zero, one, two, or three years old, I must draw the line. You are truly way too young to be daydreaming about whether you are compatible with a seventeen-year-old vampire. I am very sorry, even if you are a genius, if you are still in the cradle or in diapers or sucking on a baby bottle, then you must receive 0 points for your age. Please don't cry! Oh, okay, I'll give you 10 points for effort, how's that?

Shifting in the other direction, if you're between twenty and twenty-nine, give yourself 45 points. You shouldn't be dating a teenager, but as with the six- to twelve-year-old girls, it's probably true that you wish you could find an Edward of your own who happens to be more in your age group. In fact, I'm in a good mood, so give yourself 45 points if you're between thirty and thirty-nine, too.

Once we reach the age of forty and up, again, I must draw the line. You are too old to be hoping that you are compatible with a seventeen-year-old vampire.

And if you're over eighty years old, then shame on you, give yourself a *negative* 5,000 points for wanting to date Edward. Oh no, I hear crying again! Okay, I'll be nice. If you're over eighty years old, maybe you want to date a vampire, *any* vampire, in hopes of getting eternal life. So give yourself 10 points for effort.

Statement #1. To be compatible with someone like Edward, you need a 4 or 5. You should be sweet and caring to be with someone who is as perfect as Edward. He deserves no less!

Statement #2. To be compatible with someone like Edward, you need a 4 or 5. If you're a highly critical person, do not even try to get with a vampire dude. For one thing, keep in mind that Edward has enough self-doubts about being a vampire and leading the lonely vampire's life, so why add to his troubles? Don't criticize a guy as perfect as Edward, that's just not right. You must always be nice to him, because he deserves only the best.

Statement #3. To be compatible with someone like Edward, you need a 4 or 5. He's a complicated kind of guy, to put it mildly, so if you're not a patient person, you could end up dead. Or if you're not patient, he might avoid or leave you because your rash behavior puts his existence at risk. Also, to cope with living forever, you have to be a patient person.

Statement #4. To be compatible with someone like Edward, you need a 5, but a 3 will do, as well. "When I disagree with someone, I keep my mouth shut until I've had enough time to think about my response." Someone like Bella says what's on her mind because it takes a strong woman to be with a vampire man like Edward. So you should feel comfortable telling your man how you feel. However, there are times when you have to be careful about hurting his pride or his feelings, so if you keep your mouth shut when you disagree with him, sometimes, it might be wise.

Statement #5. To be compatible with someone like Edward, you need a 5 or a 4. Depending on your other answers, it's possible that a 2 here will not kill your chances of being with Edward. The statement is "I probably whine and complain too much." If you're with a guy this fine, you have nothing to whine and complain about, so wise up!

Statement #6. To be compatible with someone like Edward, you need a 5 or a 4. If you're often moody and depressed, you should definitely steer clear of blood-sucking vampires and their families. If you're fairly even tempered, you'll get along well with Edward. But we all get moody from time to time, so if you answered that being moody is "moderately characteristic of me," you get 2 points, and things could work out between you and Edward depending on your other answers.

Statement #7. To be compatible with someone like Edward, you need a 5, 4, or 3. The statement is, "I always tell people exactly what I think of them." The best answer is that this is "moderately characteristic of me" because sometimes, you have to tell people the truth of the matter, but at other times, it's smart to keep your mouth shut. For example, if a friend is twenty pounds overweight, you shouldn't blurt this out and hurt her feelings.

But if the same friend, who is usually very nice, one day shows up at your house and trashes your room, you are perfectly justified in telling her the truth, that her behavior is horrible!

Statement #8. To be compatible with someone like Edward, you need a 5, but you get 3 points just for being "moderately" tolerant. To be in love with a vampire dude means accepting someone who is truly different from everyone else. You have to be a tolerant person, or the relationship will never work out.

Statement #9. To be compatible with someone like Edward, you should be able to stick up for him and for yourself. This means you cannot be afraid to know what to say to people, in general. It's okay to be shy, but if you're going to lead the vampire life, you have to toughen up and learn what to say and what not to say to keep your vampirism a secret. If you're too awkward around mortal humans, it won't be safe for Edward. But because it's okay to be on the shy side, too, you get 2 points if the statement, "More often than not, it's tough for me even to know what to say to people," is "moderately characteristic to me." To be truly compatible with Edward, you should score a 4 or a 5 here.

Statement #10. To be compatible with someone like Edward, you need a 5. Here's the statement: "I crack a lot of jokes, and usually when people are with me, they laugh a lot and have a good time." A guy like Edward could probably love you whether you rate yourself as sometimes cracking lots of jokes and making people laugh, as well as always or usually being humorous. The only answer that scores anything but a 5 (and it scores a 0) is if you are never humorous and never make people laugh. Edward needs a girl who can make him smile, don't you think?

Statement #11. To be compatible with someone like Edward, you need a 5, but a 3 works, as well. If you're a total control freak, you get 0 points. But if you tend to dominate other people and get your way sometimes or "moderately," then this means that sometimes you get your way but sometimes you don't get your way. To get along with people in general, you probably need to have this type of balance. But to be with Edward doesn't require that you are a dominant person, really, so you get a score of 3 if you answered, "Not at all characteristic of me." And to be with Edward doesn't really require that you are a wallflower, so if you answered "Very characteristic of me," you also get a 3. You only get a 0 if you are a total control freak.

Statement #12. To be compatible with someone like Edward, you need a 5. You absolutely must be a loving person.

Statement #13. To be compatible with someone like Edward, you need a 5. You should always feel comfortable saying exactly what's on your mind, but we all vary a bit in our comfort levels, so every answer works except for "Not at all characteristic of me."

Statement #14. To be compatible with someone like Edward, you need a 5 or a 3. The statement is: "I am athletic and try to keep in shape." If you're going to spend eternity with a vampire who runs near the speed of light and is able to jump over tall buildings, it might be useful to keep yourself in good shape. But we all know that Bella falls and trips a lot, so Edward can be in love with a girl who isn't Miss Athlete of the Century. Hence, if you're somewhat athletic, you score 3 points. The only answer that means you are not compatible with Edward is if you answered "Not at all characteristic of me."

Statement #15. To be compatible with someone like Edward, you need a 5. Here's the statement: "When I have something to say, I speak up right away. I don't hesitate before talking." Luckily, every answer yields a 5 except for the first one, "Not at all characteristic of me."

Statement #16. To be compatible with someone like Edward, you need a 5 or a 4. If it's extremely hard for you to express yourself, then you won't say the right things when you and Edward are with mortal humans, and he could be discovered. So it's important to have enough self-confidence to know how to talk to people. If you're a little shy, that's okay, you still get 2 points. But if you're a total wallflower, it might be best to find someone other than a hunky, gorgeous, athletic, perfect vampire dude.

Statement #17. To be compatible with someone like Edward, you need a 5 or a 4. The statement is: "When things get emotional and people disagree, I have a hard time arguing for my opinion." If you have no trouble at all arguing that your emotional stance is the correct one, then you could be a hothead. Everyone's emotions differ in more than one way. On the other hand, if you never have the courage or strength to stand up for what you believe or how you feel, then you probably aren't a strong enough person to be with Edward. But anything else in between means that you and someone like Edward will probably get along.

Statement #18. To be compatible with someone like Edward, you need a 5, though a 3 works, too. Here's the statement: "I do what I want when I want to do it." If this is never true for you, or if it is always true for you, then you probably won't be compatible with many people. You can't always get your way, but on the other hand, you can't always let other people walk all over you and get their way if it conflicts with what you want.

Statement #19. To be compatible with someone like Edward, you need a 5. The statement is: "Nobody can tell me what to do." Only the answers "Very characteristic of me" and "Extremely characteristic of me" yield a score of 0. This is similar to #18. You can't always get your way, or nobody will like you very much. There must be at least a *few* people who tell you what to do, and then you listen to their advice and agree that they are right!

Statement #20. To be compatible with someone like Edward, you need a 5 or a 3. The statement is: "I go along with what other people want to do. It usually doesn't matter to me very much at all." This is slightly different from the above two statements. Here, if you do what other people want, you're easygoing and compatible with many people. It doesn't mean that you're a door-mat and that people walk all over you and take advantage of your good nature. If you answered "Not at all characteristic of me," then you score a 0.

Statement #21. To be compatible with someone like Edward, you need a 5 or a 3. The statement is: "I am an angry person." Hope-fully this is "Not at all characteristic of me," but if you get angry sometimes, that's okay, too.

Statement #22. To be compatible with someone like Edward, you need a 5, but you get 3 points just for being "moderately" toler-ant. To be in love with a vampire dude means accepting someone who is truly different from everyone else. You have to be a toler-ant person, or the relationship will never work out. This is the same as for Statement #8. For fun, see if your answer to #22 is the same as the one you gave for #8.

Statement #23. To be compatible with someone like Edward, you need 5 points. You can be extremely, very, or moderately intelligent to be compatible with Edward, but it's probably not going to work out if you have no intelligence whatsoever. Of course, Bella is supersmart and Edward is madly in love with her, but with your own Edward, maybe you can be a little less smart and still be totally adorable to him.

Statement #24. To be compatible with someone like Edward, you need 5 points. The statement is: "I am a creative person." If you're never creative at all, then you probably aren't all that interesting to hang around with, so a perfect guy like Edward won't go for you. But if you answered anything other than "Not at all characteristic of me," then you score 5 points. It's not required that you be the next Picasso or Rembrandt to be with Edward. You don't have to write award-winning poetry. But you do have to be creative enough to figure out how to get out of a lot of difficult and dangerous jams.

Statement #25. To be compatible with someone like Edward, you need 5 or 4 points. The statement is: "I am a physically beautiful person." Bella comes across as pretty but not intensely glamorous. She often comments on the physical beauty of Edward's "sisters." If you're anything from somewhat pretty to drop-dead gorgeous, Edward will probably like you. And keep in mind that very few girls fall beneath the level of somewhat pretty. If you think that you're plain, you may not be seeing yourself accurately. Ask your friends if you're physically beautiful and how they might rank you. I doubt that any of your friends will say that you look like roadkill. (If they do, then they are not your friends!)

Statement #26. To be compatible with someone like Edward, you need 5 points. You cannot be lazy if you're the girl for someone like Edward. Bella is anything but lazy. Not only does she go to school, tinker with motorcycles, and run with vampires (even to Italy!), she also cooks dinner for her father and helps take care of things around the house. If you're sometimes lazy, as many people are, then you get 2 points.

Statement #27. To be compatible with someone like Edward, you need 5 or 4 points. If you never work hard at all, then you are too lazy for Edward. If you sometimes work hard or work moderately hard, that's okay. You're still compatible with a guy like Edward. He doesn't need a workaholic. Though to be perfect for Edward, like Bella, you should work pretty hard most of the time because that's what Bella does.

Statement #28. To be compatible with someone like Edward, you need 4 or 3 points. If you're constantly overemotional, then you are not compatible with a vampire guy. You'll expose his identity and put his "life" at risk. If you're never emotional, then who would ever fall in love with you? So anything in between, any level of emotion between "nothing" and "constantly emotional" works.

Statement #29. To be compatible with someone like Edward, you need 5 points. The statement is: "I am a submissive person." You need to be able to hold your own with vampires. So if you're extremely or very submissive, forget any hope of finding or holding on to your own Edward. But any other answer works here.

Statement #30. To be compatible with someone like Edward, you need 3 points. The only answer that gets you 0 points is "Not at all characteristic of me." You have to be at least a tiny bit friendly to be with anybody. If you're bitter and cold, then nobody will want to be with you, including your girl friends.

Statement #31. To be compatible with someone like Edward, you should receive 5 or 4 points. The statement is: "Most of my friends are restless and upset a lot." If this is extremely or very characteristic of you, then you already know how to deal with strange, unpleasant, jumpy, nervous, and unpredictable people. Hence, you should do well as you travel through eternity coping with vampires, werewolves, and other undead, not to mention hysterical mortals who are attacked by vampires and werewolves. If your friends are moderately restless and upset a lot, then you might be able to cope with your new life in Edward's world. But if your friends are not at all restless and upset, then you don't have a chance coping with vampires, werewolves, and other undead: they will either eat you alive, or maybe, drink you to death.

Statement #32. To be compatible with someone like Edward, you should receive 5 points. If most of your friends are tolerant people, then you have spent your life surrounded by compassionate, understanding, decent people. They will understand when you fall in love with a guy like Edward, just as Bella's true friends understand her love for the real Edward. If it is moderately true that your friends are tolerant people, then you have been lucky to find a lot of nice friends, so you still get 3 points because many of your friends will accept your relationship with a vampire. Your tolerant friends won't expose your vampire man to people who might hurt or try to kill him. If you don't know any tolerant people, then you need some new friends!

Statement #33. To be compatible with someone like Edward, you should receive 5 points. The statement is: "Most of my friends are intelligent people." Whether your friends are intelligent or not, you are only a good friend to them if you say that they are intelligent people. What kind of friend would call her friends idiots or dummies? So if it is extremely, very, or moderately characteristic of you to have intelligent friends, pat yourself on the back: you not only receive 5 points, but you're a truly nice person, too. If, on the other hand, you claim that it is not at all characteristic of you to have intelligent friends, then you either choose your friends unwisely or you are very arrogant! Edward deserves a girl who has some humility and who treats her friends well.

Statement #34. To be compatible with someone like Edward, you should receive 5 points. The statement is: "Most of my friends are creative people." If you selected "not at all characteristic of me," then just as with the intelligence question above, shame on you! Surely, some of your friends are creative people. But if you selected any other answer, then you score 5 points. It doesn't really matter how creative your friends are. Your vampire guy is in love with you, and as long as you're creative enough to keep him happy and find ways to keep him out of trouble with mortal humans, it doesn't matter if your friends show no promise in poetry, fine art, and classical music.

Statement #35. To be compatible with someone like Edward, you should receive 3 points. The statement is: "Most of my friends are physically beautiful people." If you selected "Not at all characteristic of me," then just as with the creativity and intelligence questions above, shame on you! Surely, some of your friends are physically beautiful people. But if you selected any other answer, then you score 3 points. It doesn't really matter how physically beautiful your friends are. Edward is with you, not them. It only matters if he thinks that you are attractive.

Statement #36. To be compatible with someone like Edward, you should receive 5 or 4 points. The statement is: "Most of my friends are boring people." Clearly, the correct answer is either that this statement is "Not at all characteristic of me" or that it is "Sometimes characteristic of me." If most of your friends are boring, then you are not choosing suitable friends. If you hang out with boring people, this might indicate that you have low self-esteem. Otherwise, you would choose more interesting people to hang out with. Why should a guy who is as perfect as Edward be saddled with a girl who has incredibly low self-esteem?

Statement #37. To be compatible with someone like Edward, you should receive 3 points. The statement is: "Most of my friends work hard." It really doesn't matter how hard your friends work. A guy doesn't fall in love with you if your friends work hard or if they are lazy. He falls in love with *you*. The only poor selection here is "Not at all characteristic of me" because if all of your friends are incredibly lazy, then you either don't think much of your friends or you select friends who aren't worthy of being with you.

Statement #38. To be compatible with someone like Edward, you should receive 3 points. The statement is: "Most of my friends are highly emotional people." If it is extremely characteristic of you that most of your friends are high strung, then you are probably a livewire yourself. Maybe you're in a gang. If your friends are always weeping and wailing, then you're hanging out with the wrong crowd. In this case, you get 0 points. A fine guy like Edward doesn't need this kind of headache. On the other hand, if it's not at all characteristic of you that most of your friends are emotional people, then maybe you're hanging out exclusively with cold, unemotional robot girls. You can't be particularly compassionate and sympathetic yourself if all of your best friends are ice queens. So here, you get 0 points, too. Any other answer gives you the required 3 points.

Statement #39. To be compatible with someone like Edward, you should receive 4 points. The statement is: "Most of my friends are submissive people." To be with a vampire man for eternity requires that you have a fairly strong character. It's unlikely that Edward's perfect girl is going to hang out with a bunch of totally submissive wimps. On the other hand, we all have friends who are submissive or who are submissive from time to time, so if you chose "Not at all characteristic of me" or "Sometimes or Moderately characteristic," then you receive 4 points.

Statement #40. To be compatible with someone like Edward, you should receive 3 points. The statement is: "Most of my friends are outgoing, sociable people." It's not terribly important that your friends be outgoing and bubbly for a guy like Edward to fall in love with you. It's your personality that's going to interest him. If you're as dry as toast, never smile, never laugh, and never say anything pleasant, then you will not be compatible with Edward or most anyone else. But if you have friends who are quiet, it doesn't mean much because we all have quiet friends, fun friends, outgoing friends, and wimpy friends. We tend to have friends with different types of personalities.

Statement #41. To be compatible with someone like Edward, you should receive 5 or 4 points. The statement is: "If someone compliments a friend of mine, I feel as happy as if I had received the compliment." If you are a true friend, then you are happy when your pals receive compliments, awards, and honors. How would you feel if you received a big award or someone told you that you did better on that biology exam than anyone in the entire history of school, and then your best friend frowned and became angry at you? What if she even started muttering that it wasn't fair? You wouldn't be friends with her for very long, would you? Edward shouldn't be with a girl who acts like that. He should be with someone who is kind and generous, someone like Bella; hopefully, someone like you.

Statement #42. To be compatible with someone like Edward, you should receive 5 or 3 points. The statement is: "If someone compliments a friend of mine, I get jealous." This is similar to the last statement. You should never get jealous of a friend simply because someone compliments her. I know that we're all human, so sometimes, you just can't help feeling a twinge of jealousy, but deep in your heart, hopefully you know that it's not a cool thing. If you're a jealous witch, you get 0 points.

Statement #43. To be compatible with someone like Edward, you should receive 5 or 3 points. The statement is: "If someone insults a friend of mine, it's as if he has insulted me, as well." Clearly, you should feel bad when someone insults your friends to be worthy of a guy as perfect as Edward. So if you're never insulted when somebody makes fun of your friends, then you get 0 points. If you're sometimes or moderately insulted when somebody makes fun of your friends, then you get 3 points and you're somewhat compatible with a guy like Edward. To be truly perfect for such a perfect man, however, you should always sympathize with your friends.

Statement #44. To be compatible with someone like Edward, you should receive 5 points. The statement is: "If someone insults a friend of mine, I will stand up and defend my friend." This is very similar to the last statement. If you always or almost always stand up and defend your friends when they are insulted, then you receive 5 points. But this statement differs from the last one in a minor way. It implies that maybe sometimes you get hot-headed and always rise to the defense of any supposed insults. The previous statement simply probed to ascertain if you feel insulted when people insult your friends. In the previous statement, you didn't have to stand up and start hollering, arguing, or debating with anyone.

Statement #45. To be compatible with someone like Edward, you should receive 5 points. The statement is: "If someone insults a friend of mine, I keep my distance from the friend until things settle down." There is only one correct answer: "Not at all characteristic of me." What kind of person keeps her distance from a friend because someone has insulted the friend? This would not be a very nice person, and if you're not nice, you have no right to be with someone like Edward.

Statement #46. To be compatible with someone like Edward, you should receive 3 points. The statement is: "It matters a lot to me what other people think about my friends." Anything works here except the answer that it is extremely or very important what people think of your friends. You should care what people think about your pals, but not to the extent that it's critical to the friendships. Bella doesn't care what people think of Edward. She's in love with him no matter what other people think.

Statement #47. To be compatible with someone like Edward, you should receive 5 or 4 points. The statement is: "I would sacrifice my life to save a friend or family member." This is a very tough one to answer honestly. If you had to choose between saving the life of your little brother or yourself, if you're like most caring people, you would save your sibling. If you had to choose between saving the life of your 103-year-old grandmother or yourself, what would you do? Save your grandmother, even though she clearly doesn't have much longer to live anyway? If you selected either "Extremely characteristic of me" or "Very characteristic of me," it demonstrates that you are thinking about these various aspects of the dilemma. You have a moral conscience. We all know that Edward and the Cullen family all have moral consciences. They spare humans by draining the blood from animals, even though they hunger for human blood and claim that animal blood is akin to being vegetarians for them. So to be compatible with a guy like Edward, you need to have some pretty high morals. If your best friend was drowning, and to save her, you knew it might mean sacrificing your own life, what would you do? I would attempt to save her. If it wasn't a best friend but merely a casual friend, would you feel the same way? You get points for this one based on your answer, but the only answer for which you receive 0 points is "Not at all characteristic of me." If you wouldn't even save your little sister or your mother from drowning, then you don't deserve a great guy like Edward.

Statement #48. To be compatible with someone like Edward, you should receive 5 or 4 points. The statement is: "I would sacrifice my life to save a family member but not a friend." This is similar to the last statement, but the two statements do differ. Here, the statement suggests that you would not save your friend, but would rather save your own life than rescue him or her from drowning. But you would save a family member rather than yourself. Here, you are asking yourself whether you would help someone outside your immediate family. Hopefully, you would do what you can to save your friend, but maybe you're not sure how to answer this one so you selected "Moderately characteristic of me." If so, you get 2 points. For answers that indicate that you attempt to rescue your friends, no matter what, you receive higher points. If you wouldn't bother to help anyone, family or friend, then you get 0 points and should find yourself a guy who's a jerk rather than a good guy like Edward.

Statement #49. To be compatible with someone like Edward, you should receive 5 points. The statement is: "I would sacrifice my life if someone offered my family and friends a million dollars." Does Edward care about money and possessions? No. Sure, he drives a nice car, but for all the wealth that the Cullen family possesses, they really don't live as well as they could. In most vampire novels, the vampires live in mansions surrounded by antiques and fine paintings that they've accumulated for centuries. Most vampires dress well, look good, and live very pampered existences. They don't obtain all of their wealth by sacrificing their lives, obviously; everything simply adds up over the long stretch of their lifetimes. Edward has such high moral standards that he probably wouldn't respect a girl who commits suicide so her family can get a million bucks. It's not a very good reason for shortcircuiting a potentially wonderful life. Besides, to be with a vampire dude, you're supposed to want to live forever, right? So you can't go around committing suicide. Saving someone's life is one thing, dicing yourself for cash is quite another.

Statement #50. To be compatible with someone like Edward, you should receive 4 points. The statement is: "I believe in revenge: an eye for an eye, a tooth for a tooth." To be honest, we all think this way every once in a while. But most of us rarely think like this, and most of us rarely act with this type of impulse. An honest answer might be "Sometimes characteristic of me." If you answered "Not at all characteristic of me," then I don't believe you! Surely, somewhere along the way, you've wanted to get revenge on someone, whether you acted on the thought, or not.

Statement #51. To be compatible with someone like Edward, you should receive 5 points. The statement is: "If someone was beating up or otherwise assaulting a friend of mine, I would step in and try to fight him off, even if I'm not very strong." This is similar to a few previous questions. You should always try to help your friends.

Statement #52. To be compatible with someone like Edward, you should receive 5 points. The statement is: "I respect people who spend their lives helping other people. I would like to help people as much as possible, too." Again, to be with Edward, you should always want to help other people. Think about how many times Edward helps Bella. He saves her life over and over again. So he deserves to be with someone who is truly nice.

Statement #53. To be compatible with someone like Edward, you should receive 5 points. This statement is very similar to the last one. "If I could do something to save the world's animals from being hunted or hurt in some way, I would do it. I believe that animals suffer and have feelings, too." Hopefully, you feel this way. Edward probably feels really bad whenever he has to hunt and kill an animal. If you are with a vampire guy and are transformed into a vampire to be with him forever and ever, you will probably feel horrible about killing animals, too.

Statement #54. To be compatible with someone like Edward, you should receive 3 points. It probably doesn't matter if you think babies are cute, or not. Edward's not thinking about having babies anytime soon. He's a vampire! They don't have babies. They transform people into new vampires. So you get 3 points for this one, no matter what you answered, unless you chose "not at all characteristic of me." In this single case, you receive 0 points. If you don't like babies at all, there's something very strange about you. Even hard-hearted, mean, old curmudgeons think that sometimes, just sometimes, a baby is cute.

Statement #55. To be compatible with someone like Edward, you should receive 5 or 3 points. The statement is: "If someone gives me a gift that I don't particularly like or that I think isn't cool enough, I will make fun of the gift in front of the person." If this is not at all characteristic of you, then you are compatible with someone like Edward. And if it's sometimes characteristic of you, then you're telling the truth that sometime in the past, you've been a little mean. Maybe you even feel sorry about it now. So you get 3 points for telling the truth. Any other answer yields a big fat 0 points. If you're the kind of girl who hurts some-one's feelings simply because you want to look cool in front of someone else, then you're not being very nice. All gifts should be appreciated. It would be a lot worse if people stopped wanting to give you gifts, wouldn't it?

CHAPTER 19

THE FINAL TWILIGHT BOOK:

All the Answers You've Been
Dying to Learn

✦

Stephenie Meyer's fourth and final book in the Twilight Saga was released on August 2, 2008, and it immediately shot to bestseller status. According to *Fortune* magazine, "The last in the three-year-old, four-book series, *Breaking Dawn*, got a 3.2 million book run. In the first 24 hours after its release last Saturday, Borders (BGP) reportedly sold 250,000 copies."[1] I went to my local Barnes & Noble store at approximately noon on August 2, and they had already sold all of their copies of *Breaking Dawn*. Fans had to preorder the copies to get them on August 2. I got lucky because the store clerk took pity on me and sold a copy to me from a one-copy "stash" behind the counter: in other words, I apparently was able to purchase the only copy in the store that had not been preordered. MTV reported on August 5, 2008, that Stephenie Meyer's fourth Twilight book sold more than 1.3 million copies on its first day of release.[2]

---

1. Patricia Sellers, "Book boom: The Twilight phenomenon," *Fortune* magazine, August 7, 2008, as reported at http://postcards.blogs.fortune.cnn.com/2008/08/07/book-boom-the-twilight-phenomenon.
2. Larry Carrol, " 'Twilight' Tuesday: Stephenie Meyer Says She May Revisit 'Twilight' Universe Someday," August 5, 2008, as reported at http://www.mtv.com/movies/news/articles/1592141/story.html.

As a Twilight fan, you know how extraordinary the series is and why it is so popular. Stephenie Meyer basically became an overnight sensation. In 2003, she was an unpublished, unknown author. She was a housewife, married at age twenty-one, with an accountant husband and three sons. One day, she started dreaming of telling the story of a teenage girl who falls in love with a sweet and handsome vampire boy. She wrote her teen vampire romance novel and called it *Twilight*. Eventually, her first three novels sold more than 5.3 million copies in the United States alone. She has been a *New York Times* bestselling author for more than 140 weeks.[3]

All four of the Twilight books revolve around romantic love, and nothing sexual is found anywhere in the saga. There's plenty of kissing and swooning, and if you've already read *Breaking Dawn*, as I assume you have, you know that Bella and Edward have a child together. Yet Bella and Edward's relationship is old-fashioned, 100 percent romantic love with no "on the page" sex, swearing, drugs, or alcoholic drinking: staples in other mega-popular young adult series such as the Gossip Girl novels. Stephenie Meyer is a Mormon mother who doesn't drink alcohol herself, and she's reportedly never seen even one R-rated movie. *Time* magazine quotes her as explaining, "I get some pressure to put a big sex scene in," Meyer says. "But you can go anywhere for graphic sex. It's harder to find a romance where they dwell on the hand-holding. I was a late bloomer. When I was 16, holding hands was just—wow."[4] And *Entertainment Weekly* quotes her as saying, "I just know I'm too much of a wuss for Stephen King's books. . . . I'm *waaay* too

3. Lev Grossman, "Stephenie Meyer: A New J. K. Rowling?," *Time* magazine, April 24, 2008, as reported at http://www.time.com/time/magazine/article/0,9171, 1734838,00.html.
4. Ibid.

chicken to read horror."[5] She not only isn't into graphic sex, she also avoids horrific scenes that go anywhere beyond suggestions of raw violence. The raw sex and violence are offstage.

The good news for fans is that Stephenie Meyer may return to the Twilight Saga and further explore the relationships among Bella, Edward, and Jacob. The "final" book, *Breaking Dawn*, may actually spawn more novels in the saga.[6]

So, what's special about *Breaking Dawn*, and does it answer all of the burning questions we've had about Bella, Edward, and Jacob? Does Bella become a vampire? Do Bella and Edward get married and live happily ever after? Well, given that I've already mentioned that Bella and Edward have a baby in *Breaking Dawn*, it's obvious that the two also get married in the book.

Breaking Dawn differs from the other three novels in the series in that the fourth installment is split into three sections. The first section is told from Bella's viewpoint, the second from Jacob's viewpoint, and the third from Bella's viewpoint. I was surprised that the middle section of the book was from Jacob's viewpoint instead of from Edward's perspective. I would have been fascinated to get inside Edward's head and explore what he was thinking about Bella, their marriage, and their child. For me, as a fan, I much prefer Edward to Jacob, though other readers may very well place Jacob at the same interest level as Edward.

Bella turns eighteen years old a few days before she gets married to Edward. It's unusual in this country in 2008 for girls to get married this young, but it still happens, of course. In the case of Bella, it's really important that she marry Edward at eighteen and

5. Gregory Kirschling, "Stephenie Meyer's 'Twilight' Zone," as reported at http://www.ew.com/ew/article/0,,20049578,00.html.
6. Ibid., http://www.mtv.com/movies/news/articles/1592141/story.html.

transform into a vampire somehow. Edward's going to remain young forever, so the older Bella is before she turns into a vampire, the older she'll always be when compared to her man.

In the opening pages, we learn that Bella is engaged to Edward and the marriage is imminent. They're still in Forks, Washington, Jacob Black has disappeared from town on purpose, the cops are looking for Jacob, and Bella and Edward are still madly in love. The first fifty pages are heavy on the romance and blushing. Readers sense that something very special is about to happen, that the union of Bella and Edward will lead to her transformation into a vampire or his reversal into human form. These two are going to become cemented forever: somehow.

The wedding is spectacular, and Stephenie Meyer describes it in exquisite detail. Bella and Edward's wedding reminds me of the type of extravagant, posh events that mark the nuptials of movie stars. Except, of course, that in the Twilight case, many of the guests are vampires and werewolves! Jacob Black shows up, and a huge fight of werewolf versus vampire ensues, as he and Edward bicker over Bella. Nobody seems to notice, which I find rather odd, and the wedding reception ends up running smoothly and gloriously to its end.

About seventy-five pages into the novel, Bella and Edward leave for an extravagant and heady honeymoon on the private island of Isle Esme near Brazil. Given that my honeymoon was spent in my father-in-law's World War II pup tent at the edge of a parking lot in a state park, Bella's honeymoon totally stunned me. I would go to Isle Esme at any time, no honeymoon required.

Anyway, it is here that the couple finally consummates their marriage, which in straightforward terms means "they get it on" at long last. Edward shows remarkable restraint, considering how long it's been since he's made love to a girl. He is so deeply in love with Bella that he puts his sexual needs on hold. He's afraid that she might get hurt if they have sex. Once again, readers find that Edward is the kind of guy they'd love to meet because he has real feelings for his girl and is constantly protecting her and thinking only of her welfare. Bella insists that they have sex and she presses him for it until finally, he can't resist anymore.

The honeymoon itself is so intensely exotic that I wouldn't mind living on Isle Esme for the rest of my life. Who wouldn't want a private beach, perfect warm weather (a far cry from the gray, cloudy, rain-sopped town of Forks, Washington), ocean water that's as warm as a bath, and parrots flying everywhere? Sign me up! To make things even more enticing, visitors to Isle Esme can swim with porpoises and go snorkeling and see beautiful fish. Stephenie Meyer's description of Isle Esme is that of a tropical paradise.

Two weeks into the honeymoon, Bella becomes nauseous and tired. She has been dreaming about a tiny green-eyed child, and lo and behold, it turns out that she and Edward are expecting their first child. Edward freaks out because it's an unknown what happens when a vampire guy has a baby with a human girl. As always, Edward is consumed with protecting his beloved Bella from any harm, and who knows what kind of harm a vampire fetus might inflict on its mother? After all, it's hard enough for a human girl to give birth to an ordinary human baby. While reading, I was wondering if the baby could turn Bella into a vampire, and more significantly, if a vampire baby could actually come to term (be born without harm) inside a human mother. A normal human fetus receives nourishment from its mother's placenta. But a vampire fetus might need only iron-rich blood, and if this is the case, how does the fetus's brain and internal organs develop? These are questions yet to be answered.

At any rate, most readers probably guessed that the baby would be vampiric in some way or another, and that this factor would cause enormous complications. This entire issue is put on hold while readers plunge into the middle part of the book, which is told from Jacob Black's perspective. Here we learn that the fetus is indeed extremely strong, in fact, so strong that, as Jacob fears, it might very well kill Bella. Having given birth to two children who are not vampires, I can attest to the overall difficulty in carrying normal human babies in my "belly" for nine months. Had one of my babies been a vampire, I probably wouldn't have survived, and frankly, I am surprised that Bella's strength holds up as long as it does.

The vampire fetus is huge and developing much more rapidly than a human fetus develops. Bella is at risk and may die, as she grows increasingly weak because her human body is incompatible with the vampire fetus. A lot more happens, of course, but you've already read the book so I don't need to fill you in. While reading this fourth novel, I suspected that the story would have a happy ending because in a vampire romance, the romance is key, and if the author doesn't like horror stories, she's probably not going to opt for a gruesome ending. I figured the baby would be fine and that Edward would turn Bella into a vampire in order to save her life. I wasn't sure, of course, but these were my guesses as I rolled my way into the third and final section of *Breaking Dawn*.

It should be noted that Jacob Black imprints on the baby—which means that Jacob and the baby are bonded forever; the werewolf and the baby become soul mates—which makes Bella extremely angry. Stephenie Meyer delivers the answer to one of the key questions her fans have been asking: can a werewolf imprint on a vampire? The answer, in the Twilight Saga, is: yes.

To save Bella's life during the birth of their child, Edward injects his "venom blood" into her heart. Bella gets her wish: she is now a vampire. We watch her transformation over the course of many pages, and we're stunned by Bella's new vampiric appearance and feelings. Here, Stephenie Meyer's writing is superb, as she spins out the story of the transformation of Bella into a vampire. It is both vivid and beautiful.

The half-human and half-vampire baby girl, Renesmee, is born and grows up rapidly, showing enormous intelligence. By the age of one week, she says her first word. As I wrote earlier, a lot more happens in this fourth book, but for me, the main thrusts of *Breaking Dawn* are Bella's transformation into a vampire, the birth of her vampiric baby, and the romance between Edward and Bella. These were the areas of the plot that I cared about the most.

In the flurry of excitement following the release of *Breaking Dawn*, reports of fan disappointment have spread on the Internet. Supposedly, some readers were dismayed that Bella had a baby right after her eighteenth birthday, and others were put off by Bella's obsession with Edward. For example, Lee-Anne Goodman of the Canadian press wrote on August 9, 2008, that fans were returning books and complaining bitterly about anti-abortion messages and too strong an emphasis on Renesmee's birth.[7]

My response to these criticisms of *Breaking Dawn* is the following: first, it should come as absolutely no surprise to readers that Bella and Edward would get married early in this book. Second, it should come as no surprise that Bella has the baby early in the book. We know that Edward doesn't want to turn Bella into a

7. Lee-Anne Goodman, "Readers Protest Teen Novel 'Breaking Dawn,'" August 9, 2008, as reported at http://news.guelphmercury.com/arts/article/365065 as of August 12, 2008.

vampire. He's been refusing to do that for three books already. So we know that the only way for Edward to transform Bella is if he is forced to turn her into a vampire in order to save her life. Now, Stephenie Meyer could have chosen from a myriad of other life-threatening situations during which Edward would be forced to save Bella's life by giving her "life forever" as a vampire. She could have chosen to threaten Bella's life during a battle of vampires versus vampires or of vampires versus werewolves, just to name two very obvious examples. However, she chose a creative, new twist to the vampire theme, for which I applaud her. And, indeed, given how much Bella loves Edward, it would be against Bella's character to allow anyone to abort their unborn child. This doesn't mean that readers are getting an anti-abortion message. What readers get from all of this is that Bella, as a fictional character, chooses to give birth to what seems to be a unique infant: one who is half human and half vampire, and very much a part of both Bella and Edward.

Besides, anyone who's read the first three novels in the Twilight Saga knows that these are vampire romance novels. And traditional romance novels, vampire or not, focus on love, romance, marriage, and babies. In traditional romance novels, married women, whether they are eighteen or thirty years old, generally care more about their man than most anything else.

Of course, "modern" romances can be quite steamy and explicit, and "modern" romance heroines range from wealthy cattle rustlers to adventurous spies to gritty private detectives. But as mentioned at the beginning of this chapter, Stephenie Meyer's books are dramatically toned down from the standard fare of sex, drugs, alcohol, and mayhem found in many of the most popular young adult series.

Each reader chooses how to view Bella Swan, Edward Cullen,

Jacob Black, and the entire Twilight Saga. No matter what the stray book reviewer writes, millions upon millions of girls wish they had a guy like Edward and wish they could be Bella, if only for one day. The fan base is huge and loyal.

And, in the end, as I closed *Breaking Dawn*, the "final" book in the saga, I thought: *It's not over yet*. If anything, the story of Bella and Edward has just begun.